Simone Aliprandi

The Artificial Author

Creativity and intellectual property in the AI era

Ledizioni

Cover design by Paolo Dalprato (www.paolodalprato.com); images generated with Midjourney.

Appendix from an original work by Paolo Dalprato.

Simone Aliprandi, *The Artificial Author, Creativity and intellectual property in the AI era*
ISBN cartaceo: 9791256004898
ISBN eBook: 9791256004904
ISBN PDF Open Access: 9791256004911
Published in: september 2025

The volume is available in Open Access and can be purchased in ePub and paperback versions by Ledizioni on the website www.ledizioni.it, and in online and traditional bookstores.
Official website of the initiative: https://www.aliprandi.org/books/artificial-author/.

Indice

Introduction

In what sense "artificial author"?

The title of this book is deliberately provocative and is intended to sound somewhat like an oxymoron. We are, after all, accustomed to viewing authorship as a distinctly human prerogative and the creative act as an exquisitely human act: creative genius, creative flair, creative streak, creative work, a creative mind, a creative gift; all images closely linked to the human being. If I were to ask you outright to picture a face that embodies creativity, you would likely envision Leonardo Da Vinci, or perhaps Wolfgang Amadeus Mozart, or maybe William Shakespeare. Undisputed geniuses capable of giving birth to eternal works, which still today make our eyes shine with amazement and who remain absolute references for lovers of art and creativity. In a broader sense, however, creativity encompasses anyone who produces original work, from intellectual professionals (journalists, lawyers, architects, engineers, designers, content creators, software developers) and artisans (carpenters, potters, instrument makers, interior designers, electricians).

Before even asking ourselves what is meant by "artificial author", we must reflect on the concept of "creativity". Is it an exquisitely human act, or perhaps even divine? All the main religions, in order to provide an answer to the most primal of human concerns, that is, how the universe was formed and how life on earth was generated, have conceived fascinating narratives about various divinities who, from the height of their omnipotence and genius, created the sky, the sea, the earth, the sun, rivers, and all forms of life. Creativity therefore acquires an undeniable sacred quality, one that flows from the divine to the human realm.

Not only that: in a world where many traditionally human activities have already been delegated to machines, creativity becomes one of the last bastions of human pride, one of those characteristics that can really make a difference and help us distinguish what is the result of the automatisms of a machine and what is instead the result of human inspiration and enlightenment. But is it really still like that?

In the 2004 film "I, Robot", loosely based on Isaac Asimov's writings, Detective Del Spooner (played by Will Smith) investigates a suspicious murder that he believes was committed by a robot named Sonny. Finding himself questioning him, the detective tries to belittle him by calling him "piece of tin" and to make him face his responsibilities by asking him why he was running away. Sonny answers candidly: "because I was frightened"; and from there Spooner starts with a pressing invective, contesting that an automaton cannot feel fear, just as it cannot feel any emotion. The automaton counters by claiming to do various typically human things such as sleeping and especially dreaming. Impatiently, Spooner insists this is impossible, that only humans and animals can dream, while a robot is merely "an imitation of life"; and to support this argument, he uses the example of creativity. He asks: "Can a robot write a symphony?

Can a robot turn a canvas into a beautiful masterpiece?". The robot responds, genuinely and without sarcasm: "Can you?". A legitimate question: there are not many people who could take a canvas and paint a picture inspired by those of Leonardo. With technological evolution and in particular with the advent of digital technologies, creativity has been increasingly mediated by both hardware and software tools designed specifically to facilitate the creative process. And these tools have in turn become protagonists of creative research and related investments. The creatives of the third millennium are no longer just painters, sculptors, writers and musicians, but also video makers, software developers and designers. All this with an exponential acceleration concentrated in the last decades, precisely parallel and directly proportional to the appearance of new technologies and new forms of expression.

Among the various technologies designed to facilitate creativity, however, one has emerged that is destined to prove particularly disruptive; to the point that it forces us to rethink the very concept of creativity and therefore to question the foundations on which all legal theories of copyright rest. I am referring to generative artificial intelligence systems, that is, those artificial intelligence systems capable of creating works of the mind of various kinds (texts, images, software) with a certain degree of autonomy and following inputs that, despite being provided by a human user, are increasingly essential and concise; to the point of making us seriously doubt whether the work thus generated (the output) is truly the result of the creative inspiration of the human being who inserted the input or whether all the creative effort is assumed by the machine. And this is the fundamental question that forms the bedrock of our analysis, given that, as we will explain in more detail later, copyright has always postulated the existence of a human author and has always defined the creative character (the founding requirement of protection) according to purely human categories.

The history of this book

In March 2023, I participated as a spectator in a very interesting event organized by the Politecnico delle Arti e del Design in Florence and by ISIA Firenze, entitled "Delle Arti e nuove intelligenze" (i.e. "About arts and new intelligences"). On the stage of the Teatro Niccolini, I witnessed a thought-provoking discussion among theorists and creative professionals who enthusiastically shared their experiences with new technologies based on generative artificial intelligence, explaining how their role as authors and artists was profoundly changing in this new technological scenario.

At that time I was starting to draft the first edition of this book (which would be published in June 2023) and watching speakers present compelling examples of "syntographies" (i.e. images and animations created by using algorithms and artificial intelligence) created by AI artists truly broadened my perspective, offering me precious and concrete ideas for my writings and my university lectures.

Among the speakers at that event in Florence there was also Paolo Dalprato and from this fortunate meeting the idea was born for him to create the cover images of my book. Images that I still use today as an emblematic case study to respond to the criticism, now become a classic: "with artificial intelligence everyone is good at making images!". This view is fundamentally flawed. If it were truly that simple, I could have bypassed a creative professional like Paolo and simply experimented with prompts on my own. I am sure that the result would have been completely different and certainly not up to par.

In any case, beyond having met Paolo, that day was truly enlightening for me on many fronts: all the speakers were able to precisely identify the crucial points of the theme of "artificial creativity" and the various sessions were masterfully structured to generate that constructive dialogue and ferment of ideas necessary to address such complex and innovative themes. It is no coincidence that many of the reflections that I then developed in the book, particularly in the first chapter, began to take shape precisely by attending that lively debate in March 2023. It was clear that the paradigm was changing radically and the experts in the world of creativity were demonstrating to the audience in the room how the creative act was now deeply and inevitably interconnected with technology in many areas of artistic and cultural production.

The second version of this book has been in the works for practically a few months after the release of the first version and this English version derives precisely from the second edition. Already in June 2023 when I started giving presentations related to the first version of the book, every week I wrote down in my virtual notebook ideas and updates that I absolutely wanted to add to the pages that I had recently published. This present English version derives directly from that second, more mature and more complete version, published in Italian in May 2025.

The topic of generative artificial intelligence and all the topics connected to it ended up in the spotlight over the course of 2023 and 2024, going from niche topics to topics on everyone's lips, until they even made it into the schedules of national TV news programs, and generalist magazines, extending even to Facebook group discussions and everyday conversations at local cafés. Obviously with all the pros and cons of the waves of hype, where the pros are obviously the increase in opportunities for cultural exchange and in-depth study (presentations, interviews, lessons and conferences) and the cons are the trivializing drifts and harbingers of false beliefs, fake news and disinformation.

In just under two years, tremendous change has occurred—all at a pace that has been genuinely disorienting. The context has changed, the law has changed, the case law has changed, but above all, I have changed. In these almost two years since the release of the previous version of the book, I have met people, I have held lectures, I have participated in debates, I have answered interviews, I have edited publications and therefore I have had the opportunity to enrich myself with knowledge and ideas, I have broadened my perspective on the subject. It is no coincidence that the length of the book has essentially doubled compared to the first edition, and it could have been even greater; but at a certain point I had to set myself a limit and make a selection of the topics to discuss and the documents to comment on.

Chapter 1 – Rethinking the concept of creativity and its legal framework

1. From Greek “Techne” to Generative Artificial Intelligence: The Fascinating Evolution of the Concept of Creativity

The ancient Greeks employed the word “techne” to express the concept of “art”, cleverly linking it with the notions of “expertise”, “know-how” and “creative competence.” Many centuries later, between the eighteenth and nineteenth centuries, Anglo-American copyright doctrine established an illuminating theory whereby a work qualifies as authentically creative when three fundamental elements converge in its creation: “skill, labor and judgement”. Here we find, with surprising relevance, an echo of the “creative skill” of the ancient Greeks: the ability to choose the most suitable chisel to sculpt marble, the art of skillfully mixing oil colors to spread them effectively on canvas, the skill in harmoniously orchestrating instrumental parts to compose an engaging symphony.

During the twentieth century—or perhaps as early as the final decades of the nineteenth—the ancestral concept of techne in creative fields became increasingly intertwined with the modern notion of “technology.” Innovative forms of creativity emerged that could not do without technological support: from photography, with its revolutionary mechanical processes (think of the seminal court case of Napoleon Sarony's photo of Oscar Wilde, quoted extensively in this book), to digital graphics and electronic music, all the way to our own times, times in which the vast majority of creativity is necessarily expressed through software and algorithms. Today, with the exception of the more traditional arts such as sculpture, painting, and the choreographic arts, all creative forms transit, in whole or in part, through digital tools: writing in all its declensions, contemporary music composition, photography, cinematography, advertising and editorial graphics, industrial design, interface and service design, architecture, and software development. These activities are predominantly executed via computers or other increasingly sophisticated digital devices (tablets, professional cameras, cutting-edge smartphones), employing specialized software designed for specific purposes.

In the past few years, however, we have taken another significant leap forward, definitively entering a new technological and creative era. Generative artificial intelligence systems no longer represent mere passive tools in the hands of authors, but take on an increasingly complementary and surprisingly purposeful role. Starting from human input, these systems are able to come up with innovative and totally unexpected solutions, opening up previously unimaginable creative scenarios.

The creative process still remains initiated and controlled by the human being, but a significant part of "skill" and "labor" is assumed by artificial intelligence. The human being is undoubtedly left with the "judgement": the fundamental creative choices about the input to be provided and the careful selection of the output to be published and disseminated as a completed work. The human being accurately determines the direction of the generative process and judges with artistic sensitivity when the output fully meets his or her creative needs, deciding the appropriate time of its "crystallization" into a work usable by the public. Expertise transforms and adapts to the new paradigm: traditional skills specific to each artistic form are no longer exclusively required, but the importance of "fine tuning" of the AI system emerges overwhelmingly. Conscious choice (judgement) becomes the indispensable cornerstone of the new creativity, allowing authors to proudly claim "I created this with AI" instead of just passively saying "this was generated by AI".

Of course, all this holds true only when the human user genuinely adopts a creative mindset; it certainly does not apply in cases where we passively allow the machine to operate independently, accepting whatever initial output it generates, perhaps by relying on pre-compiled prompts.

Nevertheless, it is undeniable that within this complex and rapidly evolving landscape, the author's role is undergoing a profound transformation—one so radical that many copyright scholars struggle to formulate new and appropriate interpretative paradigms. Classical copyright law, which emerged in the eighteenth century during the era of literature, painting, and symphonic music and was predicated on the inescapable assumption that an author must be human, now reveals clear conceptual and practical limitations. How can a markedly "human-centered" legal institution adapt to a world in which creativity is deeply intertwined with technology and in which there is increasing talk of an author "hybridized with the machine"?

The legal world will inevitably need its physiological time to develop adequate responses to these challenges, and it will be my endeavor to keep interested audiences constantly updated on these developments. In the meantime, it seems essential to develop an in-depth and systematic reflection on the role of the author and its rapid evolution in this new technological revolution, which even from its earliest beginnings shows us the extraordinary speed of the changes taking place and those to come. Can we already begin to speak concretely of a "hybrid author" or a "meta-author", as some visionary thinkers have begun to suggest?

2. Authors not human but not artificial either: the parallelism with works created by animals

During my teaching and outreach activities, when discussing non-human creations, I often draw a parallel that invariably evokes curiosity and sympathy: the comparison with works created by animals.

2.1. Most emblematic cases

Chronologically, the first documented case raising questions about the protectability of such works emerged in the early twentieth century with paintings partially created by a donkey named Lolo. The term 'partially' is significant here: the donkey was largely guided by a human artist through fundamental steps such as color selection and brush placement. Furthermore, the artist himself (Frenchman Roland Dorgelès) subsequently modified the sketch produced with the animal's assistance, thereby making a substantial, if not decisive, creative contribution.

An early documented case of works created autonomously by animals, albeit with human encouragement and assistance, is that of Congo, a chimpanzee who began making pencil scribbles on paper at just two years of age and eventually produced approximately four hundred drawings and paintings, including in color, with some of them exhibited at the Institute of Contemporary Art in London. His abstract and Surrealist-style works were explicitly appreciated by the likes of Picasso (who had one hanging in his house), Dali and Miró, and over the years they were also auctioned off for very high sums.

Then there is the story of Pigcasso, a sow painter originally from South Africa who is known for being the first animal to have her own exhibit and for signing her works with an imprint of her nose.

Impressive are videos of some trained elephants able to pick up a brush with their trunk and draw a stylized image of an elephant on the canvas. In this case, however, there are ethical doubts about the ways (probably cruel or otherwise not respectful of the animal's nature) in which such elephants were trained to behave in this way.

Finally – saving the best for last – a case where the art of the animal is perhaps less refined but the copyright debate is instead very heated (and still open): the famous Monkey Selfie in which a female cynopithecus (more commonly, macaque) appears to be smiling while taking a photographic self-portrait. The story dates back to 2011 when nature photographer David Slater, during a photo shoot in an Indonesian nature reserve, allowed several macaques to "play" with his equipment. The result went beyond expectations, as one of these animals took two photos of itself that closely resemble what we now call a "selfie", and in one of them it even appears to be smiling. Slater released these images, highlighting them as the first "animal selfies" in history, and they garnered significant attention; however, he soon encountered an unexpected copyright dilemma. Can the photographer really claim a copyright on those images for merely owning the equipment and setting it up in the park for the macaques to use? Perhaps not. The fact is that those photos have been reproduced over and over again by various sites, including those of the Wikimedia Foundation (Wikipedia, Wikimedia Commons), as public domain images and therefore free of any constraint, angering Slater who has taken legal action (so far remaining ineffective) and has never shown any acceptance of the situation.

But why can this parallelism with "bestial creations" help us better understand the problem of the relationship between generative artificial intelligence and copyright? Because even then, the underlying doubt is much the same: can the animal or the machine own copyright? We could also leave the question far more general and broad and ask whether they can be rights-holders, but then we would probably enter into a very intellectually stimulating discourse that cuts across philosophy, but which risks getting out of hand and losing the focus of this book.

Staying on the level of copyright, the question then becomes whether a nonhuman entity that is not aware that it is performing a creative act can become the holder of a copyright or even a more generic right of use. The jurists' answer on the copyright of creations made by animals has been quite nimble and hasty: an animal cannot own a copyright because copyright is strictly a human matter. On the other hand, the animal painter, although brilliant compared to his peers and amazing in our eyes, does not perform a real creative act because he is driven more by a kind of instinct, a curiosity towards the creative tool (the brush, the paper, the camera), a tendency to play or because he is trained by human beings to replicate creative clichés (as in the case of elephants); but still he is not moved by a conscious creative impulse.

The animal is thus regarded as a mere agent of nature that makes possible something that the human eye perceives as pleasing, curious, and artistic, but which is not true creative work in the sense intended by copyright. A bit like the sounds, sometimes really pleasant and almost musical, created by the wind when it brushes against Pinuccio Sciola's sculptures or the often harmonic and musical sounds produced by the sea breaking over Nikola Bašić's so-called Sea Organ in Croatia. Can we say that the wind and the sea hold a copyright on these sounds? And can we perhaps say that Sciola and Bašić also hold rights of use over the sounds produced by their works? Obviously not.

Some have used the "sweat on the brow" theory (more on this later) to argue, as in Slater's case with the macaques, that even if the man did not directly create the work he still went out of his way to create the situation that led the animal to create; and this "going out of his way" should still somehow be protected with a right of use in favor of this man, perhaps not a copyright in the proper sense but something more like a related right[1]. But even this argument has been shown to be weak.

Incidentally, in some jurisdictions (even those in which case law precedent has binding force) there have been rulings that have precisely ruled out the possibility of attaching a copyright to animals. And as we shall see in the next section, even the United States Copyright Office (henceforth also USCO) has taken a clear position on the issue, expressly excluding the protectability of works created by animals, but also by other agents of nature, by any non-human agent and even by the Holy Spirit (yes; this is not a joke, it is precisely one of the examples used in official documents).

2.2. Non-human creations and the clear position of the U.S. Copyright Office

Precisely in order to settle the doubts raised by the Monkey Selfie case and the subsequent lawsuits brought by photographer Slater, the U.S. Copyright Office (USCO) in 2014 wanted to expressly clarify[2] its position in an updated edition (the third) of its

1 Related rights (or neighbouring rights) are exclusive rights normally attributed to subjects who do not have a real role as authors but who contribute significantly to the creation or diffusion of the works (for example: producers, performers).

2 See Jacob Axelrad, *US government: Monkey selfies ineligible for copyright*, 22 August 2014, https://www.csmonitor.com/Technology/Tech-Culture/2014/0822/US-government-Monkey-selfies-ineligible-for-copyright.

Compendium of U.S. Copyright Office Practices[3]. The paragraph in question (Sec. 313.2) deals not only with creations made by animals but more generically with all works that lack human authorship, and is in fact entitled "Works That Lack Human Authorship". Because of its importance and centrality, we quote it in full in an Italian translation slightly paraphrased to make it more understandable and then make some comments.

> «As discussed in Section 306, the Copyright Act protects "original works of authorship". To qualify as a work of "authorship" a work must be created by a human being. See Burrow-Giles Lithographic Co., 111 U.S. at 58. Works that do not satisfy this requirement are not copyrightable.
>
> The U.S. Copyright Office will not register works produced by nature, animals, or plants.
>
> Likewise, the Office cannot register a work purportedly created by divine or supernatural beings, although the Office may register a work where the application or the deposit copy(ies) state that the work was inspired by a divine spirit.
>
> Examples:
>
> • A photograph taken by a monkey.
> • A mural painted by an elephant.
> • A claim based on the appearance of actual animal skin.
> • A claim based on driftwood that has been shaped and smoothed by the ocean.

3 The original document is available at https://copyright.gov/comp3/docs/compendium.pdf.

> • A claim based on cut marks, defects, and other qualities found in natural stone.
> • An application for a song naming the Holy Spirit as the author of the work.»

And so far we are talking about works created (assuming we can use the verb "create") by natural entities. The USCO document, however, goes on to a terrain that instead is much closer to the one we are exploring with this book. In fact this is what it reads:

> «Similarly, the Office will not register works produced by a machine or mere mechanical process that operates randomly or automatically without any creative input or intervention from a human author. The crucial question is whether the 'work' is basically one of human authorship, with the computer [or other device] merely being an assisting instrument, or whether the traditional elements of authorship in the work (literary, artistic, or musical expression or elements of selection, arrangement, etc.) were actually conceived and executed not by man but by a machine.
>
> Examples:
>
> • Reducing or enlarging the size of a preexisting work of authorship.
>
> • Making changes to a preexisting work of authorship that are dictated by manufacturing or materials requirements.
>
> • Converting a work from analog to digital format, such as transferring a motion picture from VHS to DVD.
>
> • Declicking or reducing the noise in a pre-existing sound recording or converting a sound recording from monaural to stereo sound.
>
> • Transposing a song from B major to C major.

- Medical imaging produced by x-rays, ultrasounds, magnetic resonance imaging, or other diagnostic equipment.

- A claim based on a mechanical weaving process that randomly produces irregular shapes in the fabric without any discernible pattern.»

As early as 2014, a few years before the spread of generative AI systems, the USCO thus posed the question of works generated by a mechanical and automated process whose output is not dictated by human choice but rather by randomness. In particular, pay attention to the following words, which effectively condense the true essence of our reflection:

> «The crucial question is whether the 'work' is basically one of human authorship, with the computer [or other device] merely being an assisting instrument, or whether the traditional elements of authorship in the work [...] were actually conceived and executed not by man but by a machine.»

3. Machine-mediated creativity: a historical problem for copyright law

Today, no one would doubt that photography is a kind of art. Major museums of modern and contemporary art have entire sections devoted to photography, and those who normally enjoy artistic content cannot fail to appreciate that form of creativity as well. And even when photography does not manifest itself in its highest, most original and stylistically refined form, but is limited to documenting reality, there is no doubt that it is nevertheless understood as one of the expressive forms of human beings. All over the world, in fact, intellectual property laws grant photography protection, sometimes as a copyright in the proper sense, sometimes as a related right.

However, photography emerged during the first half of the 19th century and gained widespread popularity in subsequent decades, thus postdating the establishment of copyright law. Within the community of jurists, the question therefore arose as to whether that new form of expression could be considered a creative form in the proper sense and thus be brought within the scope of copyright law. The doubt, which to us in the new millennium might seem strange or unfounded, was in fact entirely legitimate.

Until that time there had never existed a creation so dependent on a machine and in which much of the work was done by the machine; or at least so it seemed to the first people who actually encountered the problem. These naturally included publishers and printers who wanted to reproduce photographs in their books, newspapers, and magazines. In an effort to serve their own interests, they argued that photographs were not the product of creative acts but merely the result of mechanical processes; after all, it was enough to own a camera, position it and activate it. Consequently, according to this interpretation, photographs were freely usable and reproducible without having to account to those who had enacted that mechanical process (the photographers, that is).

This was essentially the argument presented by a printer who found himself defending his position in court, inadvertently setting the stage for one of the most revolutionary rulings[4] in American copy-

4 The text of the decision is available at https://supreme.justia.com/cases/federal/us/111/53/.

right history. This was the case decided by the U.S. Supreme Court on March 17, 1884 to settle a dispute that had arisen between photographer Napoleon Sarony and the Burrow-Giles Lithographic Company, which had marketed lithographic reproductions of a (now very famous) photograph of writer Oscar Wilde taken by Sarony and titled "Oscar Wilde No. 18".

The Supreme Court essentially upheld the interpretation reached by the lower court according to which

> «[Sarony], by posing the said Oscar Wilde in front of the camera, selecting and arranging the costume, draperies, and other various accessories in said photograph, arranging the subject so as to present graceful outlines, arranging and disposing the light and shade, suggesting and evoking the desired expression, and from such disposition, arrangement, or representation, made entirely by the plaintiff, produced the picture in suit.»

In this way the Court came to conclude that the photographer was in all respects "the author of an original work of art" and therefore his activity must legitimately fall within those things for which the Constitution permitted the granting of exclusive rights under copyright laws.

Why is this case law so revolutionary and why do we still find ourselves citing and commenting on it today? Because on the one hand it establishes that photography is not a mere objective reproduction of reality because, depending on the person behind the camera and on the creative choices he makes (light, framing, background, setting) and the indications he gives to the subject portrayed, the image will be different and may even denote the photographer's personal point of view, his style and creative approach.

On the other hand it confirms that even what requires the support of a machine is creative, which obviously brings with it a certain level of automation. It all depends on evaluating how high the level of automation is compared to the result obtained; that is, whether three different photographers equipped with the same equipment and positioned in front of the same subject would actually be able to take three almost identical photos or whether, on the contrary, each would produce something different. In the end, therefore, it would be confirmed that what matters is not the tool used or the technical process applied, but the way in which the human being has used the tool and applied the process, thus becoming an author in all respects. Here, we can in a certain sense say that the debate that arose at the end of the nineteenth century regarding the protectability of photography is being re-proposed today – albeit in different ways and contexts – regarding the protectability of creations made through generative artificial intelligence systems.

Aside from cases of unsupervised generative artificial intelligence systems with a large degree of "creative autonomy" (a fascinating phenomenon that we will discuss later in a specific paragraph), we tend to talk about works created with AI systems and not by AI systems. It is the human being who provides the input to the machine and reworks the output to bring it ever closer to the desired result; it is the human being who decides whether the output provided is suitable for publication or, on the contrary, whether it requires further reworking and adjustments; it is the human being who decides in which venues the output will be published and who takes responsibility for it. In this perspective, therefore, generative AI systems, even if they really are something capable of seriously undermining copyright, still manage to be brought back under its scope.

Ultimately, it seems like we are seeing scenes already seen: in the 1980s there were those who said that electronic music, being made with sequencers, samplers, software, was not real music because it was not really composed by humans but programmed with the computer. Yet today no one would deny the creative character and, at certain levels, the artistic value of that type of music. The same goes for multimedia graphics and digital animation: in the 1990s there were those who argued that it was not true visual art, because in reality the artist was not really drawing but was only giving instructions to specialized software. Even in that case, no one would now doubt that it is a well-rooted and widespread form of human creativity.

But until when will this be the case? How long will AI systems need to be guided and trained by humans to generate good quality works? Will we be able to use the same approach even when human input is truly reduced to the mere "press a button and choose the image you prefer"? And beyond the ontological investigation on how to qualify this type of activity (creative or compilation?), how should we frame this new phenomenon from the point of view of intellectual property law?

Another interesting perspective is the one proposed by Wingströma, Hautala and Lundman in their article "Redefining Creativity in the Era of AI? Perspectives of Computer Scientists and New Media Artists"[5], in which they show that this type of reflections is older than it may seem; and it must be considered that the article dates back to 2021 (published in 2022) therefore well before the advent of the popular generative AI platforms. Many authors have already questioned the evolution of the concepts of creative and author linked to the appearance of increasingly high-performance and autonomous technologies for the creation of intellectual works. Even the anxiety of being replaced by machines in one's role as creative is not so new and remains an effect of the scant knowledge of how generative AI works. In fact, the article states:

> «Some research has suggested that human evaluators tend to be negatively biased toward art generated by AI, as opposed to art made by humans (Ragot, Martin, & Cojean, 2020). People might lack understanding of AI, or creativity might be perceived as a uniquely human trait. The idea of independently creative AI means a "competitive relationship" between humans and AI and evokes questions as to whether AI could replace humans as a creative actor (Gioti, 2020, p. 25). The abilities of AI in creativity processes are very different from those of a human. Humans mobilize their skills into a versatile spatial creation process and, for example, respond to their culture, create meaning, move in different environments, engage in social interaction, build tools, or test new ideas. Although AI can simulate some of these skills, it cannot combine creative skills like humans can (Hertzmann, 2018, p. 19).»

---

5 Roosa Wingström, Johanna Hautala & Riina Lundman, *Redefining Creativity in the Era of AI? Perspectives of Computer Scientists and New Media Artists*, in *Creativity Research Journal*, 2024, VOL. 36, NO. 2, 177–193 (p. 182), DOI https://doi.org/10.1080/10400419.2022.2107850.

4. A human-centered copyright

This book addresses a method of creation and artistic expression that is genuinely novel, one that many would have considered unimaginable just a few years ago. Yet the revolution is already in progress, and we are undeniably moving toward what might be called "post-human creativity". And with it we will need a copyright that is no longer strictly anthropocentric.

As we have already emphasized extensively, artificial creativity presents us with new questions for copyright and is perhaps one of the most arduous challenges for legal science. How can we frame this new phenomenon in which the role of the human being is becoming increasingly marginal and that of the machine (more precisely, of the algorithm) is instead becoming central? And how can we respond to this challenge if all the cardinal principles of this legal institution for the last three centuries have been consolidated around the human being?

For those in Anglo-American jurisdictions, who are more accustomed to the concept of "copyright", this transition may prove less disruptive. Since 1988, British law has included the concept of computer-generated works (also abbreviated as CGW), with the Copyright, Designs and Patents Act (CDPA); a concept to be distinguished from computer-assisted works, that is, works created by a human being with the assistance of a computer. But surely in 1988 no law maker could have imagined the scenario that has arisen in recent months.

For those who operate in systems inspired by the French model, the issue could be even more complex, given that we are not talking about copyright but rather about "author's right", that is the set of all the rights of the person who creates the work. The human being is at the center, starting from the etymological level. Roberto Caso, in his 2021 writing on the relationship between copyright and artificial intelligence, highlights the problem in an extremely effective way:

> «Author's rights and in particular moral rights (like other personality rights) are human-centered. They were developed with humans in mind. Although many copyright laws, including the Italian one, do not define the founding concepts of author, creativity (originality), expression (expressive form) and work, there is no doubt that they were conceived in a technological era that did not know AI. The adaptability of these concepts is relative.»[6]

The final point of the extract on the limited adaptability of certain legal concepts is truly enlightening. A point that inevitably projects us towards the need for new paradigms and probably new rules that can better frame the phenomenon of "artificial creativity".

5. The idea of creativity for legal theory

The excerpt from Roberto Caso's essay rightly reminded us that the founding concepts of author, creativity, and originality do not find a precise definition in the law; in fact, they have been defined more

6 Roberto Caso, *Intelligenza artificiale e diritto d'autore*, chapter 22 of *La società della mercificazione e della sorveglianza: dalla persona ai dati*, Ledizioni, 2021.

by case law (i.e. the principles applied by judges in sentencing) and even more in detail by doctrine (i.e. the articles and comments of legal scholars).

Let us therefore try to clarify and understand how those key concepts are considered in the legal field.

First of all, a premise is necessary. For the sake of terminological clarity and consistent with this book's informative purpose, I am treating the terms "copyright" and "author's right" as though they were synonymous and direct translations of each other. To be frank and greatly simplify matters, we are discussing two distinct legal institutions that are rooted in different juridical contexts and have emerged from separate historical trajectories: on the one hand, the Anglo-American copyright, mostly widespread in the countries of the former British Empire; on the other hand, the French copyright, mostly widespread in the countries of the former Napoleonic Empire. Copyright (literally 'the right to make copies') focuses primarily on reproduction rights, usage rights, and their commercial value; whereas author's right aims to protect creativity on both 'moral' and reputational levels through specific personal rights that complement economic utilization rights. These two "brothers", while retaining their distinctive characteristics and differences, have gradually converged through various international conventions, as well as through digital interconnection, market globalization, and the proliferation of standardized contractual models. In both approaches, one of the doctrinal pillars is the identification of what should fall under the protection of copyright or author's right; and to this end the laws and jurisprudence of the various legal systems have developed a solid set of principles in order to establish what should be considered creative and therefore worthy of protection, and what should not.

5.1. The idea of creativity in Italian law

In Italian copyright law (as well as in other legal systems derived from the French model), creative character constitutes the fundamental requirement for copyright protection. Without at least a minimal degree of creative character, the work either receives no protection whatsoever (placing it in the public domain) or falls under protection that cannot be classified as full copyright, and therefore may be protected by a related right or another right (such as, for example, the sui generis right on databases). The Italian law on copyright (Law 633/1941) mentions the creative character in its first article and thereafter, but does not provide a definition. We must therefore look to case law and legal scholarship for guidance.

Traditionally, according to Italian legal theory, a work is considered creative if it is sufficiently original and new. Schematically, we could therefore say:

creative character = originality + novelty

Originality refers to the outcome of substantive human ingenuity and intellectual effort that reveals the author's personality. Although we have thus arrived at a greater level of detail, we have not yet definitively clarified the concept; moreover, even the adjective "non-trivial" lends itself to various interpretations, which can be influenced both by subjective aspects (i.e. the level of competence and experience of the person who must evaluate the creative contribution) and by the context and historical moment in which the creative activity in question takes place. We must also acknowledge that over the decades judges have tended to lower the bar in the evaluation of originality, recognizing creative character even in works whose creative contribution was quite negligible and therefore very close to "trivial".

The concept of novelty also requires clarification. From an objective standpoint, legal precedents frequently define it as the presence of essential and distinctive elements that differentiate the work from prior creations. As legal scholar Giovanni d'Ammassa[7] briefly explains,

> «According to other scholars, novelty should not be understood in an absolute sense but must be tempered, since it is easy to recognize even in works of the highest caliber the trace of previous creations of others, as the author benefits from his own cultural heritage and his own experiences as a perceiver (novelty in the subjective sense). It follows that the work is endowed with a creative character when it bears the imprint of the author's personality, reflecting his personal way of representing and expressing facts, ideas and feelings, and presents individual characteristics that reveal the contribution of a specific author.»

5.2. The concept of creativity for Anglo-American copyright

Anglo-American jurists approach this differently. As previously mentioned, they refer to a threshold of originality comprised of three elements: skill, labor, and judgment. "Skill" indicates creative competence,

7 See https://www.dirittodautore.it/la-guida-al-diritto-dautore/loggetto-del-diritto-dautore/.

knowing how to do something in a creative way. "Labor" indicates the commitment, the effort, the time needed to create a work of the mind; in more colloquial terms, "the effort" that the author has made to create the work. Finally, "judgment" refers to the ability to discern and select the distinctive aesthetic and content elements of the work.

The presence of just one of these requirements is not sufficient to invoke copyright protection. Undoubtedly, the mere presence of labour without a minimum of skill and judgement cannot be sufficient, although there is a theory called "sweat of the brow doctrine" according to which whoever uses resources, time and effort to create something (even if not particularly original) still has the right to have this investment protected[8].

On the basis of what we have already said regarding the "non-triviality" of the creative contribution, Anglo-American case law (in particular Canadian)[9] has also had the opportunity to specify that the exercise of skill and judgement would require intellectual effort and "must not be so trivial that it could be characterized as a purely mechanical exercise".

The expression "purely mechanical exercise" brings us back to our basic question, that is, whether a work created by a machine or in any case with substantial support from a machine can be considered creative. Using the conceptual categories of Anglo-American

8 For more details on this topic, see https://en.wikipedia.org/wiki/Sweat_of_the_brow.

9 On this case law orientation see the case *CCH Canadian Ltd. v. Law Society of Upper Canada* decided by the Supreme Court of Canada and the case *Feist Publications v. Rural Telephone Service* decided by the Supreme Court of the United States.

law, we can say that it is precisely judgement that represents the strongest basis for considering works produced with AI systems protectable by copyright. In a context where software contributes both skill and labor, human beings retain the crucial power of judgment. In fact, it is the human being who gives input to the AI system, to judge whether the output provided is in line with their creative idea, with their style; it is the human being who establishes whether the output obtained is worthy of being published as it came out or whether it needs adjustments and improvements; it is the human being who chooses among the various outputs proposed by the system which is the best and most suitable to be used and distributed. It must also be considered that the applicable forms of protection are not limited to copyright in the strictest sense, because related rights can also play a fundamental role. Consider, for example, musical works created with AI systems that are subsequently developed into complete commercial recordings. In that case, the level of related rights of the phonographic producer and of the performing artists overlap. A similar argument can also be made for the sui generis right of the maker of databases, in the case of databases created with AI systems.

FOCUS

Creativity for the world of law

- Anglo-American legal systems (copyright)
  → *skill + labour + judgement*

- European legal systems (author's right)
  → *originality + novelty*

6. "It's not art! It's just statistics"

When discussing generative artificial intelligence and "AI art", one of the main criticisms often heard can be summed up as: if it's not human, it can't be art! This brings to mind the scene from the film "I, Robot" where Detective Spooner interrogates the android.

The detective, adopting a contemptuous attitude, berates the android, dismissively calling it a mere "piece of tin" created by humans and programmed to imitate them. Similarly today, when artificial intelligence theorists seek to temper the often apocalyptic rhetoric surrounding the debate, they remind us that ultimately, these systems are nothing more than statistics, albeit a highly refined form of statistics.

> «But what›s inside AI? Nothing. Well, to be precise, nothing "intelligent", just statistics. Highly sophisticated statistics, impressive computer architectures, and remarkable transformers operating within intricate neural networks, but no actual thought. [...] Word relationships aren't processed semantically but merely in terms of positional proximity [...]. Generative Pretrained Transformers (GPT) do only one thing: starting from a received text (input) they guess (choose randomly from a set of most probable words) the next word. And that's it, except that they repeat this process recursively until they form a complete text to be displayed (output). Recursively means that each new "guessed" word is added to the original text forming a new input from which to "guess" the next word and so on. Take-home message: zero intelligence. But it works.»

This is what physicist Andreas Formiconi[10] said; effective and enlightening, as well as lapidary and brutal. Zero intelligence that, however, works and is increasingly entering the use of intellectual activities. If there is no intelligence, can there ever be creativity? Answer: it depends. It depends a lot on what we mean by "creativity".

As any attentive reader will have noticed, in these first paragraphs of our discussion we have spent many words to give a more defined form to the concept of creativity, at least from the legal point of view; however, we have not dwelt on the concept of art. We could launch into an extensive discourse on what constitutes "true art" versus mere creative exper-

---

10 Andreas Formiconi, *AI generativa, stato dell'arte, (fosche) previsioni — spero sbagliate ma a pensare male...*, 9 September 2024; https://iamarf.org/2024/09/26/ai-generativa-stato-dellarte-fosche-previsioni-spero-sbagliate-ma-a-pensare-male/.

imentation, but such a discussion would likely prove interminable and, more importantly, lies beyond the scope of this work. Here it is appropriate to underline that, for the purposes of a legal argument on the protectability of works created with artificial intelligence systems, it is of little importance whether they are art in the noblest sense of the term. Copyright is concerned not so much with artistic works per se, but rather with creative works more broadly; it makes no qualitative or stylistic judgments. Among the types of works that are traditionally subject to copyright protection, there are also works that have very little of an artistic nature, such as software, databases, literary works of an educational and technical nature, or maps and documentary photographs. Consequently, a volume of poetry by a renowned poet and a dry political economy handout receive identical copyright protection; both are classified as literary works (under Article 2 of the Bern Convention) with their authors entitled to precisely the same rights.

The jurist's investigation must therefore focus on the presence of a creative character (as we have already explained above) and must not extend to evaluations of the artistic value, unless it is a work of industrial design.

According to the Italian Copyright Law, in fact, the only type of works in which not only the presence of the creative character but also that of the artistic value is relevant are industrial design objects: clothing and fashion accessories, jewelry and costume jewelry, furniture, tools, technological devices, car bodies, motorcycles, boats, and the like. For this type of creation there is already a form of protection more similar to that of the patent, therefore based on the filing of the design at a specific office and payment of a fee to obtain protection. However, Italian law stipulates that design projects of particular significance demonstrating artistic value also qualify for full copyright protection. Through this legal pathway, Italian case law has established a framework for defining what constitutes "artistic" in legal terms.

In my lectures, especially to design students, I try to explain this topic by citing a ruling from the Court of Appeal of Milan that had to decide on a case of marketing of furniture (armchairs and sofas) that were imitations of those designed by the famous French architect Le Corbusier. The Milanese judge[11] had the opportunity to define what the artistic value of a work can consist of (in general) and to indicate how it can be identified for the purposes of recognizing copyright protection for a design object.

> «The recognition of the "artistic value" of a work [...] can only derive (at least initially) from an evaluation made by the community of enthusiasts, experts in the individual branches of art, who very often act as "trailblazers" for the recognition then attributed by the community of citizens. This judgment must develop over a sufficient period of time, beyond temporary trends and passing enthusiasms. The attribution of the value of a "work of art" to a work (as history teaches) at the beginning is very often the result of a judgment of culturate people, particularly competent both in the specific artistic branch, and in the socio-cultural currents that the artist is inspired by and of which the work is an expression. This occurs especially when a work breaks the patterns and canons

11 See the decision by Corte di Appello di Milano (sentenza n. 1716,18 Aprile 2013), in the case *Cassina c. Alivar and Galliani Host Arredamenti*.

> previously followed and, consequently, not understood by the mass of the public, but appreciated by enlightened critics. That said, when a work is exhibited in museums or non-commercial art galleries, one cannot dismiss the fact that it has been recognized as a "work of art" by the critical community and by those with cultural expertise in the field (not to mention refined aesthetic sensibilities).»

What often confuses people encountering this explanation is that the recognition of a design object as a genuine work of art, rather than merely "ordinary" design, inevitably occurs retrospectively. The designer creates the chair, the lamp, the bag, the car model with the idea of creating something aesthetically pleasing and innovative; and only later, on the basis of the impact and reception that his creation has obtained, it rises to the status of a work of art.

Now that we have some more specific references on the concept of "artistic value" (always understood in a legal sense), we can trace everything back to the creation of works with generative artificial intelligence systems. It is illogical to dismiss these creations as non-art simply because they are generated by AI systems. In any case, recognition of artistic value would occur later, through the assessment of individuals with particular sensitivity and expertise in the field (and in legal disputes, by judicial evaluation).

How does American case law define the concept of "art"? First, it should be noted that there is no single, all-encompassing statutory or judicial definition of "work of art" under U.S. law. However, courts and tribunals have addressed the issue in various contexts, primarily in relation to copyright and tariffs on works of art.

Key points that emerge from U.S. case law are as follows:

- Broad interpretation – Courts tend to adopt a broad interpretation of what constitutes a work of art, going beyond traditional forms such as painting and sculpture.
- Author's intent – The author's intent in creating the object is often considered a relevant factor. If the primary intent is aesthetic, conceptual, or emotional expression, it is more likely to be considered a work of art.
- Public perception – How the object is perceived by the public may also be relevant. If it is generally regarded and appreciated for its aesthetic qualities, this may support its classification as a work of art.
- Originality and creativity – As with copyright in general, the work must exhibit a certain degree of originality and creativity to be considered a work of art in some legal contexts.
- Specific context – The definition of "work of art" may vary depending on the specific legal context in which it is applied (e.g., copyright, import, tax).[12]

In summary, while there is no single definition, U.S. case law tends to consider a work of art as a creative expression, made with the intent to elicit an aesthetic or conceptual response, and that is perceived as such by the public. The precise definition may vary depending on the specific legal context.

Derek Fincham's in-depth analysis on the topic is also very interesting:

12 This list was compiled with the help of Gemini AI.

> «Defining art is hard, and the variety of artistic expression cautions us against an overly-limiting definition. A universal definition of art might start with the idea that art is an expression of the creator meant to convey value, emotion, commentary, or instill some feeling or idea in the viewer. More precise definitions may be formulated of course, but this gives us a rough idea of what the concept of art could be for the law moving forward. The important thing to note at the outset is the way in which the law does not start at the center of a definition. Anyone agrees of course that a canvas by Claude Monet or a sculpture by Michelangelo are art. The law serves a function at the outer limits, resolving disputes which may arise and deciding what is art and what is non-art incrementally. [...] As conceptual and contemporary art pushes boundaries, the law will invariably distinguish art from non-art.»[13]

7. It's all about autonomy

As our discussion has revealed thus far, the central issue hinges on the degree of "creative" autonomy these systems possess. As long as generative artificial intelligences are mere tools (albeit very powerful) at the service of the human being and under the control of the human being, there are not many doubts on the level of management of usage rights since we would remain on the path already marked by other technological revolutions that have brought new forms of creativity previously unknown (photography, electronic music and multimedia graphics for example). However, if we think in perspective, we must in fact

13 See Derek Fincham, *How Law Defines Art*, 14 J. MARSHALL REV. INTELL. PROP. L. 314 (2015).

begin to enter the perspective of AI systems that will assume ever greater creative autonomy, leaving the human being in an increasingly marginal role and reducing the intellectual contribution also in terms of judgement. This scenario could really take the phenomenon outside the scope of copyright, or at least copyright as we have understood it up to now.

Regarding the level of autonomy of these systems, it is useful to recall the distinction between strong artificial intelligence and weak artificial intelligence. Without delving too deeply into Turing's work or the science fiction of Asimov, Cameron's Skynet (Terminator), or Ridley Scott's "I've seen things you people wouldn't believe..." (Blade Runner), it's worth noting that artificial intelligence has been a topic of discussion for decades, so it's hardly a recent phenomenon. The idea of being able to artificially create something that has an ever greater degree of autonomy in connecting information and responding to external stimuli triggers many fantasies and perhaps even a certain fear; and in recent years the further scenario that we are discussing in these pages has emerged: that is, the application of artificial intelligence to the world of creativity and art. This last scenario is the one that could start to bring us closer to the concept of strong artificial intelligence, because generative AI systems in creating works based on very essential inputs would assume ever greater "creative autonomy" by proposing increasingly refined aesthetic/narrative solutions and making the creative contribution of the human being increasingly marginal (which, as we have explained, would be limited to the level of judgement).

Let's read the explanation provided by Paolo Marinoni[14] on the conceptual differences between strong AI and weak AI:

> «Weak artificial intelligence is the one we all know and which has as its objective the creation of systems that can correctly perform some complex functions typically human. In this case, the machines do not possess a degree of intelligence equal to or superior to that of humans, but simply imitate the behavior that a human being would have for the execution of a specific task. It is therefore a 'simulated' and not real intelligence. [...] This kind of AI is therefore created to solve more or less complex problems and, to do so, is trained by humans through a learning phase based on feedback. However, the use of neural networks and deep learning suggests that machines have the potential to perform even more complex tasks.
>
> Strong artificial intelligence, on the other hand, does not see the machine as a simple problem-solving tool. According to this theory, an intelligent system could

14 See Paolo Marinoni, *AI debole e forte: differenze concettuali e limiti*, https://ainews.it/ai-debole-e-forte-differenze-concettuali-e-limiti/. Please also read the explanation provided by the official IBM website: «Weak AI, also known as narrow AI, focuses on performing a specific task, such as answering questions based on user input or playing chess. It can perform one type of task, but not both, whereas strong AI can perform a variety of functions, eventually teaching itself to solve for new problems. Weak AI relies on human interference to define the parameters of its learning algorithms and to provide the relevant training data to ensure accuracy. While human input accelerates the growth phase of strong AI, it is not required, and over time, it develops a human-like consciousness instead of simulating it, like weak AI. Self-driving cars and virtual assistants, like Siri, are examples of weak AI.» Source: https://www.ibm.com/think/topics/strong-ai#.

in fact achieve a cognitive capacity similar to or even superior to that of humans.»

The fact that an artificial intelligence is able to create something aesthetically refined and exciting, without any particular indications from a human being, is truly a fundamental distinction; especially if the creation of the artificial author is not easily distinguishable from that of a human author. That is precisely the turning point indicated by Turing.

In a disquisition made with the focus of copyright like ours, rather than talking about strong AI and weak AI, it is even more central to distinguish between supervised AI vs. unsupervised AI.

There are several experimental projects aimed at showing that these systems can – in a certain sense – be "left free" to see what they are able to generate even without any supervision from a human being.

An illustrious example is the artistic installation Unsupervised designed by Refik Anadol[15], a Turkish-American new media artist and designer, and exhibited in the entrance hall of the MOMA in New York. Abstract images generated by the system flow seamlessly across a large screen, allowing viewers to observe the installation in motion while standing, or seated on purpose-built benches. The system has been operating continuously since the installation was positioned and started, without the artist or any of the museum staff intervening.

15 See the official website https://refikanadol.com/works/unsupervised/.

Figure 1: Anadol installation at MOMA in New York (photograph taken by Simone Aliprandi in August 2023).

Francesco Bardozzo (aka Oberlunar) pursues similar creative-musical experiments. In his writings and conference presentations, he discusses unsupervised artificial intelligence and – with somewhat provocative intent – the concept of the meta-author.

> «From composer he becomes the creator of a composer equipped with artificial intelligence. [...] Let's imagine a computer with enormous computational power. [...]

> Oberlunar trains his creature by feeding it (he says exactly that) musical notes without imposing rules. Like any self-respecting creator, he leaves free will to his composer so that the music generated is without human rules, without history and therefore different. That newness that disorients.»[16]

The musical pieces of this "artificial musician" provoke very different reactions among the various listeners; as always, much depends on how elastic the ear of the listener is and how open it is to new and unusual sound experiences. But it is interesting to note that, by conducting the famous Turing Test on these musical works (i.e. the test that tries to understand how much an artificial intelligence can "camouflage" itself with human intelligence), few have been able to recognize them as non-human.

The concept of machines capable of autonomous creation dates back further than most would expect. There are in fact two quite famous examples of machines capable of producing graphic works and paintings: AARON, developed by Harold Cohen since 1973, and The Painting Fool, developed since 2001 by Simon Colton. Both systems, despite their initial, more modest objectives, can now autonomously generate full-color paintings. Harold Cohen himself describes his machine's output thus:

> «AARON, is creative? With no further input from me, it can generate unlimited numbers of images, it's

16 See Giusy De Vitis, *Se l'intelligenza è artificiale, la musica è vera?* (the article contains an interview with Oberlunar), 21 October 2021, https://www.filodiritto.com/se-lintelligenza-e-artificiale-la-musica-e-vera.

a much better colorist than I ever was myself, and it typically does it all while I›m tucked up in bed.»[17]

AARON, in particular, has received a lot of attention after being included in a Windows screensaver by Kurzweil CyberArt Technologies, Inc.[18]

Also on this topic, the aforementioned article by Wingström, Hautala, and Lundman is useful. They argue that computational creativity has two major perspectives that lead us to distinguish between "independently creative AI" and "co-creative AI"; and for each of the two categories they provide several very interesting examples.

«The first perspective focuses on developing AI that simulates human-level creativity (Colton & Wiggins, 2012). For instance, machine learning techniques can be used to classify neural markers of divergent thinking ability (Stevens & Zabelina, 2020) or problem-solving (Colin, Belpaeme, Cangelosi & Hemion, 2016). [...] The second perspective of computational creativity focuses on developing AI that is co-creative with humans. Human–AI co-creativity aims to blend the creativity of humans and AI in an interactive process "on a shared task in real time" [...].»[19]

17 Harold Cohen, *Driving the creative machine*, Orcas Center, Crossroads Lecture Series, 2010, https://www.aaronshome.com/aaron/publications/orcastalk2s.pdf.

18 On these topics, see also the Wikipedia entry "Computational creativity".

19 Roosa Wingström, Johanna Hautala & Riina Lundman, *Redefining Creativity in the Era of AI? Perspectives of Computer Scientists and New Media Artists*, in *Creativity Research Journal*, 2024, VOL. 36, NO. 2, 177–193 (p. 182), DOI https://doi.org/10.1080/10400419.2022.2107850.

8. Towards a new form of authorship

The experiments of Anadol, Oberlunar, and other AI artists compel us to reconsider the traditional conception of authorship and abandon the strictly anthropocentric perspective that has dominated for centuries (and continues to permeate legal literature). However, the so-called crowdsourcing had already paved the way for the crisis of the concept of the author understood in the classical sense, as a human subject who expresses his creative inspiration in full autonomy and solitude. In large crowdsourced projects we see that the role of the author is transfigured with that of a member of a community of authors and can take on different nuances (contributor, reviewer, validator and/or commentator). Now the advent of generative artificial intelligence poses a further level of complexity: the human author tends to almost merge with the machine which, however, has in turn been trained with human-derived content.

8.1. Shared authorship and crowdsourced works

In recent history, even before the question of "creative machines" was raised, we had already seen a paradigm shift in the approach to creativity and authorship. I am referring to a phenomenon that has absorbed my attention throughout the first years of my humble career as a popularizer and independent scholar and which concerns creative projects of undoubted revolutionary value, such as the GNU/Linux operating system and the free encyclopedia Wikipedia.

The role of the individual author dissolves, giving way to a kind of macro-authorship embodied by the user community. In technical terms, this is known as crowdsourcing, which emphasizes the "crowd" element: a diverse collective of individuals, operating without centralized direction and receiving no compensation for their intellectual property contributions, yet voluntarily – and often enthusiastically – participating in the creation of two complex, sophisticated intellectual works that have become fundamental to our contemporary world. On the one hand, the most well-known open source operating system, widespread in millions of computers, smartphones, devices and household appliances, and that we all use sometimes even unknowingly; on the other hand, the most consulted encyclopedia in the world, the most primary source of information from which the same search engines and artificial intelligence systems draw to provide an initial answer to our questions.

On these topics there is a vast and interesting literature dating back to the decade between the end of the nineties and the beginning of the new millennium, of which I would like to point out three popular works that were of great enlightenment for me in those years of my education.

The first is the short essay "The Cathedral and the Bazaar" written by Eric Steven Raymond in 1997 and then republished in various versions and translations[20]; it is considered one of the reference texts of hacker culture and the open source world. The work, telling the story of the first and most important free software projects and in particular of the Linux kernel, reflecting on the philosophical and

20 Its most recent English version dates back to 2000 and is freely available (under the Open Publication License) at http://www.catb.org/~esr/writings/cathedral-bazaar/.

ethical assumptions, welcomes a new model of software development, collaborative and decentralized (the bazaar), in contrast to the more traditional and centralized one (the cathedral).

The second work is perhaps the one most focused on the theme of collaborative creativity and is in fact entitled "Wikinomics. How Mass Collaboration Changes Everything", released in 2006 in the original version. The authors Don Tapscott and Anthony D. Williams are inspired by the unexpected and recent (for the time) success of the project to create the largest free and shared encyclopedia: Wikipedia, precisely. A mammoth and revolutionary work, child of the crowdsourcing model, in which a new approach to authorship is effectively realized; contributors in fact voluntarily choose to adhere to the rules of the community, to participate in the "wiki" writing project (sometimes even completely anonymously) and to pour their creative activity into a larger, undefined, continuously evolving entity (precisely, the community of contributors). In Tapscott and Williams' book, the example of Wikipedia and in general of the Wikimedia Foundation's projects become the starting point for a series of reflections, also on new business models and new economies based on the online sharing of knowledge and creative experiences.

The third work in chronological order (2008) is by a scholar whom I have had the opportunity to meet twice in person and who represents a sort of master for those who deal with my themes: Lawrence Lessig. And the book in question, among the many fundamental books that have come from his pen[21], is enti-

21 In particular *The Future of Ideas: The Fate of the Commons in a Connected World* (2001) and *Free Culture: How Big Media*

tled "Remix: making art and commerce thrive in the hybrid economy". In the work, Lessig comes to terms with a fact that according to him can no longer be ignored by the economy, by law, by politics: the effects of the spread of digital technologies and the web on the world of creativity and the cultural and entertainment industry. In fact, they have brought new forms of creativity based inevitably on the sharing of creative works and on their reuse and re-elaboration (the remix, precisely). In this form of creativity, even the role of the authors changes, becomes blurred, each one participates by adding a piece and arrives at a new and interesting creative result "standing on the shoulders of his peers"[22].

8.2. Hybrid authorship and the concept of meta-author

Returning instead to the revolutionary impact already exerted by the advent of generative artificial intelligence, some authors have already pointed out that a new form of creativity is now asserting itself in which the work necessarily arises from an interaction between the human being and the machine and the figure of the author himself emerges transfigured and blurred.

An absolute precursor of this idea was Douglas R. Hofstadter who already in his book "Gödel, Escher,

Uses Technology and the Law to Lock Down Culture and Control Creativity (2004).

22 This sentence is one of the key passages of the video *Get creative* that illustrates in a super-effective way the spirit of the Creative Commons project. The video is available at https://creativecommons.org/about/videos/get-creative/.

Bach" dating back to 1979[23] had theorized the existence of a "meta-author" referring to the very first software for programming electronic music. In the eighteenth chapter, dedicated precisely to some "retrospectives" on artificial intelligence that take their cue from Turing's theories, he writes:

> «The distinction between author and meta-author is sharply pointed up in the case of computer composition of music. There are various levels of autonomy which a program may seem to have in the act of composition. One level is illustrated by a piece whose 'meta-author' was Max Mathews of Bell Laboratories. He fed in the scores of the two marches 'When Johnny Cornes Marching Home' and 'The British Grenadiers', and instructed the computer to make a new score – one which starts out as 'Johnny', but slowly merges into 'Grenadiers'. [...]. In Mathews' own words, "this is a nauseating musical experience but one not without interest, particularly in the rhythmic conversions". [...] The resulting piece has a somewhat droll quality to it, though in spots it is turgid and confused.»

He then continues his reflection by asking the question that underlies this entire chapter: is the computer creating that music? And trying to construct an answer, he points out that the result of that automated process (while far removed and very different from that of current generative AI systems), can be "pleasantly surprising".

> «Is the computer composing? The question is best unasked, but it cannot be completely ignored. An

23 Douglas R. Hofstadter, *Gödel, Escher, Bach: an eternal golden braid*, Basic Books, 1979 (Chapter XVIII, *Artificial intelligence: retrospects*; paragraph *Who composes computer music*), https://archive.org/details/GEBen_201706/.

answer is difficult to provide. The algorithms are deterministic, simple, and understandable. No complicated or hard-to-understand computations are involved; no "learning" programs are used; no random processes occur; the machine functions in a perfectly mechanical and straightforward manner. However, the resuit is sequences of sound that are unplanned in fine detail by the composer, even though the overall structure of the section is completely and precisely specified. Thus the composer is often surprised, and pleasantly surprised, at the details of the realization of his ideas. To this extent only is the computer composing. We call the process algorithmic composition, but we immediately re-emphasize that the algorithms are transparently simple.»

As we have already mentioned above, Francesco Bardozzo (aka Oberlunar) has repeatedly taken up the concept of meta-author in his conferences and writings. In addition to being a scholar of artificial intelligence on a technological level, he is also a musician who in art goes by the name of Oberlunar and who loves to experiment with the new possibilities of musical composition brought by generative AI systems.

In his contribution to the book "La musica del futuro. Lo scenario artificiale" (i.e. "The music of the future. The artificial scenario") edited by Roberto Manfredi[24], Bardozzo recalls Hofstadter's theory and writes:

«According to Hofstadter, the meta-author is the creator of an artificial intelligence that in turn produces an artistic work. [...] Despite the considerable limitations

24 Francesco Bardozzo, *Generazioni generative italiane*, in Roberto Manfredi (editor), *La musica del futuro. Lo scenario artificiale*, Tempesta Editore, 2023 (pp. 86-87).

of modern technology, in the end my perseverance won out. Therefore, I decided to move the level of abstraction of my artificial intelligences, moving from the simple reading and prediction of sequences of notes in a score to more philosophical and intrinsic rules in musical logic. I began by introducing the concepts of consonance and dissonance, as well as the concept of Augustine's actus sentiendi, which I believe concretely regulates the perception of the relationships between sounds over time. Subsequently, I explored concepts of sequence and semiotics [...].
It was clear that a machine would never be able to deconstruct, given its capacity for interpolation rather than extrapolation. However, if it had been able to deconstruct the score and had adopted a training approach other than those based exclusively on supervised examples [...], it could still have offered something interesting.»

With an even more structured and in-depth approach, Paolo Dalprato has dedicated an entire essay to the topic entitled "Hybrid Creativity. Author and Work in the Era of Intelligent Machines", in which, using examples related to the visual arts, he invites us to look at new forms of creativity and art linked to artificial intelligence with curiosity and open-mindedness and shows us that the process of "human-machine hybridization" in the creative field has been underway for much longer than one might think.

Hybrid authors are therefore already among us and the contribution of software and algorithms is already an integral part of various forms of creativity. Dalprato writes:

«What I call "hybrid author" is a figure that embodies the synergy between the technological capabilities of

> AI and the human artistic vision, creating a bridge between the world of traditional art and the frontiers of technological innovation. The hybrid author is a new paradigm in the collaboration between humans and machines in the field of creativity. This collaborative model paves the way for the expansion of the boundaries of human creativity, offering new creative horizons.»[25]

Dalprato takes us into this world by showing the various ways in which humans can interact with generative AI and recognizes what had already been reported almost 50 years ago by Hofstadter, namely that generative artificial intelligence in providing us with its outputs often surprises us positively, offering us ideas and showing us creative paths that we would not have considered on our own. Dalprato goes a step further and identifies the phases of this new form of creativity based on human-machine interaction:

> «The interaction between humans and artificial intelligence develops through three fundamental phases: input, generation and selection. These phases, through iterative cycles, lead to the desired result. Taken together, they represent the moment of the actual generation of the image, but they are preceded by a crucial phase: the definition of the project. It is at this moment that the idea is born and takes shape in the author's thought.»[26]

Dalprato's reflection, among other things, seems really in line with what emerges from the article by Wingströma, Hautala, and Lundman regarding

---

25 Paolo Dalprato, *Creatività ibrida. Autore e opera nell'era delle macchine intelligenti*, Ledizioni, 2025 (Chapter 2, Paragraph 2.4).

26 Paolo Dalprato, *ibidem*.

the concept of "co-creative AI"; in particular in the following passage:

> «Research has shown that AI is capable of generating new ideas and inspiration for humans, providing knowledge that enhances humans' creative abilities, overcoming fixated thinking and "blank canvas paralysis", and inspiring individuals by presenting sketches of varying similarity.»[27]

8.3. A new way of creating... and thinking?

Some authors have hypothesized a new form of creativity that we could define as artificial creativity, or computational creativity, or even algorithmic creativity. Among these authors, it is worth mentioning first of all the English scholar Geraint Wiggins who speaks of computational creativity and defines it as:

> «The study and support, through computational means and methods, of behaviour exhibited by natural and artificial systems, which would be deemed creative if exhibited by humans.»[28]

In Italy, an excellent work of dissemination and philosophical reflection on the theme of algorithmic creativity, with a particular focus on graphic and figurative arts, is conducted by Francesco D'Isa. Among the first in Italy to experiment with the creation of

---

27 See R. Wingströma et al., *Redefining Creativity in the Era of AI? Perspectives of Computer Scientists and New Media Artists*, in *Creativity Research Journal*, 2024, VOL. 36, NO. 2, 177–193 (DOI https://doi.org/10.1080/10400419.2022.2107850). p. 182.

28 Geraint A. Wiggins, *Searching for computational creativity*, in *New Generation Computing*, vol. 24, n. 3, 2006, pp. 209-222.Francesco D'Isa, *La rivoluzione algoritmica. Arte e intelligenza artificiale*, Luca Sossella Editore, 2024

graphic works with extensive support of generative artificial intelligence (such as his graphic novel Sunyata published in 2023), in the book "La rivoluzione algoritmica. Arte e intelligenza artificiale" (i.e. “The algorithmic revolution. Art and artificial intelligence”)[29] he invites readers to explore how artificial intelligence is redefining the boundaries of artistic expression and intellectual property.

But if we want, we can go even further and leave the mere field of creativity and hypothesize a new form of thought, brought about by this increasingly constant human-machine interaction. Someone has spoken of a real “cognitive revolution”, and this “someone” is a group of Italian researchers who in 2024 published an important article in the scientific journal Nature entitled “The case for human-AI interaction as System 0 thinking”. They argue that “data-driven AI systems, transcending individual artifacts and interfacing with a dynamic and multi-artifact ecosystem, constitute a distinct psychological system” and that they are changing the way humans make decisions. The authors follow the path of previous theories by Daniel Kahneman[30], who in one of his essays had spoken of “System 1” and “System 2”, and call this new cognitive system “System 0”. According to Kahneman, System 1 represents fast and intuitive thinking and System 2 slow and analytical thinking. System 0 would instead represent the outsourcing of some cognitive tasks to AI, which can process large amounts of data and perform complex calculations

29 Francesco D’Isa, *La rivoluzione algoritmica. Arte e intelligenza artificiale*, Luca Sossella Editore, 2024.

30 Daniel Kahneman, *Thinking, Fast and Slow*, Straus and Giroux, 2011.

beyond human capabilities. This concept emerges from the dynamic interaction between users and AI systems, creating a personalized and adaptable interface between humans and information. Based on Clark and Chalmers' extended mind hypothesis[31], System 0 is seen as an extension of the human mind, enhancing both intuitive and analytical thinking.

Of course, the integration of System 0 raises important epistemological and ethical questions, as we increasingly rely on AI-mediated decision-making processes that we do not always have full awareness and control of, with all the biases and risks that this entails.

We find an illuminating perspective on this topic in Daniel Susskind's renowned essay "A World Without Work"[32]. Chapters 3 and 4 of this work guide us through the historical evolution of AI, revealing what some authors call the "fallacious approach to AI", or more simply, the "AI fallacy"[33]. For decades,

---

31 Andy Clark e David J. Chalmers, *The Extended Mind*, in *Analysis*, vol. 58, n. 1, January 1998, pp. 7-9.

32 Daniel Susskind, *A World Without Work. Technology, Automation, and How We Should Respond*, Metropolitan Books, 2020.

33 Susskind takes these theories from a previous book written in collaboration with his father Richard and entitled *The Future of the Professions: How Technology Will Transform the Work of Human Experts* (Oxford University Press, 2015). As Rachel Muller-Heyndyk reports for HR Magazine, Daniel Susskind, speaking at the Learning Technologies 2019 conference, declared: «The general approach towards artificial intelligence [...] was the same; if you wanted to build a machine that could outsmart a human expert you had to sit down with an expert, get them to explain to you how they solved the problem, and then try and capture that human explanation in a set of instructions or rules for machines to follow.» See Rachel Muller-Heyndyk, *Daniel*

AI researchers believed that the most sensible and effective way to create machines that could perform certain tasks with high proficiency was to imitate human beings as closely as possible: observe humans who excel at performing that task, translate their operations into instructions comprehensible to a machine, and then impart those instructions to the machine. Only in a second phase of AI research (from the 1990s onward) did they realize that this approach was not necessarily the winning one. The author explains that, according to the more traditional approach, machines can equal or even surpass humans only in "routine" tasks, precisely because these are more easily observable in human practice and can be synthesized into instructions to be given to the machine. "Non-routine" tasks, however, are those that require tacit knowledge—that type of knowledge that people struggle to express clearly and which therefore can hardly be synthesized into a series of instructions. A classic example is the so-called "clinical eye" of an experienced physician, that intuition which enables the doctor to understand from a glance, a smell, or an unusual movement that the patient is unwell. Another example, one that more closely concerns the reflection of our book, is creative inspiration, which allows the painter, musician, or poet to produce something truly original, innovative, and emotionally engaging.

The theory that "the only way machines can be intelligent is through replicating human skills" proves to be highly misleading. A more mature approach by scientists has demonstrated that artificial intelli-

---

Susskind: The AI fallacy, 18 February 2019, https://www.hrmagazine.co.uk/content/news/daniel-susskind-the-ai-fallacy/.

gence has its own different way of tackling problems and performing tasks; therefore, attempting to reduce everything to the typical categories of human thought leads us to lose focus, engage in fallacious reasoning, and dangerously underestimate the capabilities of machines. According to Susskind, we must accept that there are various ways of being intelligent; machines can demonstrate intelligence that differs from human intelligence, but is no less remarkable or performant for that reason. He explains this by recounting one of the most classic stories: that of the IBM computer which in 1996 first demonstrated its ability to defeat chess champion Garry Kasparov.

> «[Kasparov] was blown out of the water by its super high-processing capabilities and very high storage. The system was playing a very different game to him, and when we spoke to one of the founding fathers of AI for our book he summed it up by saying: 'there are lots of ways of being smart that aren't smart like us'.»[34]

Kasparov himself, in his written narrative of those chess matches played against the Deep Blue software[35], acknowledges the conceptual trap into which we often fall. He states that as soon as humans find a way to make a computer do something intelligent (such as playing chess at world championship levels), we then decide that this is not true intelligence and that human beings possess other, more authentic characteristics for being considered intelligent.

The same should apply to the concept of creativity. We tend to consider creativity as a quintessentially human characteristic; however, perhaps we should

---

34 Rachel Muller-Heyndyk, *ibidem*.

35 Kasparov, G., *Deep Thinking: Where Machine Intelligence Ends and Human Creativity Begins*, PublicAffairs, 2017.

accept that there can be different ways of conceiving creativity beyond the more traditional one. In his book, Susskind urges us toward precisely this reflection and recounts a truly illuminating episode. As early as 1997, at the University of Oregon, a large group of spectators listened to a piano piece, believing it to be an authentic composition by Bach; in reality, that work had been created autonomously by EMI, software developed by composer David Cope. Susskind[36] aptly observes that if a human being had written that musical work, we would not have hesitated to use the word "creative". Nevertheless, the idea of defining that act as a creative act met with some reluctance. And we often forget to recognize that machines, even if they cannot reason like a human being or have creative inspiration like that of a human artist, might nonetheless be capable of completing tasks that we would normally define as creative if accomplished by human beings.

9. Law is late and technology makes the rules

The legal world has always had difficulty regulating new technological phenomena. This is because technology progresses at a much faster pace than the laws that regulate its use. Furthermore, to establish the rules of a particular phenomenon, the legal world needs that phenomenon to manifest itself and stabilize. "Preliminary" regulatory interventions, attempts

36 Daniel Susskind, A World Without Work. Technology, Automation, and How We Should Respond, Metropolitan Books, 2020 (Chapter 4, "Underestimating machines").

to regulate future or developing technologies, never work and indeed risk having the (counterproductive) effect of stifling the growth of those technologies; after all, as Tim O'Reilly effectively points out, "you can't regulate what you don't understand"[37].

Let's take an example. In recent years I often find myself giving lectures or writing articles on what is commonly called "the new copyright directive", i.e. directive 2019/790. New because it is in fact the latest EU directive approved in the field of copyright, with the ambition of regulating the protection and use of creative works for at least a decade or perhaps even more. The one immediately preceding it dated back to 2001; it therefore took 18 years for a change of pace. And the 2019 directive is in any case "new" also in the sense that national legislators took all the time available (about two years) to approve the transposition laws; in some cases even more time than necessary, as happened in Italy where the implementing decree appeared in November 2021 and some regulations even in the second half of 2022. So basically

37 *You Can't Regulate What You Don't Understand. Or, Why AI Regulations Should Begin with Mandated Disclosures* is the title of a well-known blog post by the popularizer and publisher Tim O'Reilly published on 15 June 2023, a few days after various controversies related to the regulation of artificial intelligence. The post reads: «Regulators should start by formalizing and requiring detailed disclosure about the measurement and control methods already used by those developing and operating advanced AI systems. In the absence of operational detail from those who actually create and manage advanced AI systems, we run the risk that regulators and advocacy groups "hallucinate" much like Large Language Models do, and fill the gaps in their knowledge with seemingly plausible but impractical ideas.» See https://www.oreilly.com/radar/you-cant-regulate-what-you-dont-understand/.

it is new; its impacts are not yet fully understood and there is already talk of some corrective interventions to fix some aspects not regulated in a sufficiently clear and linear way.

Well, to write these pages I found myself consulting various articles on the topic of artificial intelligence dating back to the years 2019-2020, that is, almost contemporary with the directive that we still call "new"... and they seemed prehistoric, now obsolete, out of context. Yet they are authors who usually show great foresight.

In addressing this problem, common law legal systems (i.e. those inspired by the Anglo-Saxon model) are undoubtedly more advantaged than civil law systems (including Italy and the European bloc in general). Simplifying the issue a bit, we can say that the former, in the hierarchy of sources of law, give more importance to case law, that is, to the stratification of principles established by courts and tribunals with their sentences; the latter, on the other hand, give greater centrality to legislation, that is, to legal texts and regulations. In modern and functioning jurisdictional systems in which trials do not last years but at most a few months, case law undoubtedly has faster reaction times than legislation which must respect the times of the so-called iter legis ("the path of the law"), which on the most complex and politically sensitive issues can drag on for years (and let's go back to the example of the Copyright Directive which was discussed in 2016 but was implemented by the Member States not before the beginning of 2021).

The collateral effect is that case law can show greater reactivity and flexibility in regulating new and controversial legal issues, working more on the stratification and sedimentation of principles and, at the same time, being able to allow a certain level of legal "creativity", in the sense of the possibility of creating new legal principles to respond to a given case (as happened with the example of Oscar Wilde's photograph).

This gap between technology and law becomes even more evident with the spread of artificial intelligence[38]. The challenges that artificial intelligence presents to the world of law are many and do not only concern the aspect of intellectual property (which is the focus of this book). Indeed, other aspects seem to raise greater concerns and are not yet adequately regulated: among these we certainly find that of data privacy, civil liability for the "actions" of AI systems and the safety of people who use such systems. Very indicative is the fact that it was the creators and promoters of AI systems themselves who pointed out the need for more precise and timely regulation[39].

Indeed, the history of the European regulation on artificial intelligence, commonly known as the AI Act

---

38 In this regard, it is interesting to refer to the concept of technological neutrality in point 7 of the European Parliament Resolution of 20 October 2020 on intellectual property rights for the development of artificial intelligence technologies, which states: «[Parliament] considers also that the Union must address the various aspects of AI by means of definitions that are technologically neutral and sufficiently flexible to encompass future technological developments as well as subsequent uses». Full text is available https://www.europarl.europa.eu/doceo/document/TA-9-2020-0277_EN.html.

39 Among the various statements by the big names in the sector, we point out the most famous: the tweet by Sam Altman, founder of OpenAI: «we definitely need more regulation on ai» (available at https://x.com/sama/status/1635136281952026625).

(and more precisely Reg. 2024/1689/EU), becomes even more emblematic, approved in its final form in the spring of 2024 but starting from a first draft dating back to 2021. As if that were not enough, the entry into force of the regulation is staggered in phases that will only conclude in mid-2026, when the AI Act will be fully operational. In the meantime, EU member states will also have to approve various national regulations aimed at establishing specific control activities, defining technical standards and assigning tasks and responsibilities. All this in a sector that every six months or so is capable of seeing disruptive innovations capable of changing even regulatory needs. In this scenario, I seem to notice that, in the very first months following the fateful release of ChatGPT (October 2022), the most concrete answers to the legal questions posed by the spread of generative artificial intelligence systems did not come from legislators, who felt bogged down and disoriented by the speed of diffusion of these systems and their potential impact on various human activities. They did not even come from judges who had not yet had many opportunities to deal with concrete cases. They came mostly from theoretical jurists, from legal scholars, that is, from the so-called legal doctrine; but they also came from the lawyers of the pioneering companies in the sector, who were called upon to draft the terms of use of the various platforms and the guidelines for correct use.

The result is that technological rules essentially override legal rules approved by democratic institutions, and they do this on a global scale, leveraging economic power and often disregarding existing laws as they are deemed no longer adequate to keep pace with technological innovation. Moreover, this occurs with a shift in tax revenues and, more generally, a concentration of wealth in one part of the world (California), to the detriment of other regions' economies.

This is a problem that has already manifested with significant impact in the social media era and now, in the artificial intelligence era (an even "faster" and more disruptive technology), risks having even more devastating effects on the legal and economic world.

10. The focus on liability

Among the various legal issues posed by the advent of AI systems, that of copyright management has emerged more recently (as it is linked to the generative platforms that had their "explosion" at the end of 2022), and has remained quite in the background compared to that of civil and criminal liability for the "actions" (if we want to call them that) of devices with a high degree of automation.

In other words, the main concern has always been to define who should be held civilly, criminally and administratively liable for what comes from artificial intelligence. The classic example: if a self-driving car causes damage to things or people, or simply violates the highway code, who is responsible? The company that created the AI system that governs the car? Or perhaps the person who "put the car on the road" without providing correct settings or without checking whether there were particular conditions on that road? Or even, in a future with many self-driving cars, the public body that manages that road and has not updated the signs, confusing the car's AI system?

Or, to give some examples that bring us back to the law of information and intellectual property, who is liable for any defamation caused by a news article written with an AI system? And again, who is liable for copyright infringement in the case of a piece of music created and distributed by an AI system, which however is very, too similar to a pre-existing piece?

Even the EU regulation on artificial intelligence and the resolutions connected to it seem to focus more than anything else on this aspect of liability. In particular, read the European Parliament resolution of 20 October 2020 with recommendations to the Commission on a civil liability regime for artificial intelligence[40]. A "risk-based" approach emerges from the European legislator with a consequent classification of AI systems based on the risks they pose to fundamental rights. The systems considered high risk and the specific requirements to which they must comply are identified, as well as the obligations for AI providers and users belonging to this category[41].

Although in a different way, the terms of use of the main generative artificial intelligence services also do not miss the opportunity to underline that the responsibility for the content created and its use, as well as for any copyright infringements, must fall on the user and not on the service provider. We will see this more clearly later.

---

40 The full text is available at https://eur-lex.europa.eu/legal-content/EN/TXT/?uri=oj:JOC_2021_404_R_0006.

41 For more details see the *EU AI Act Handbook* written in 2025 by White & Case LLP and available at https://www.whitecase.com/insight-alert/white-case-launches-eu-ai-act-handbook.

11. An ethical issue too (or perhaps mainly)

Beyond legal considerations lie ethical and deontological concerns. Since law cannot anticipate and regulate every possible scenario, we must foster among users of these tools a commitment to proper, honest, and transparent usage that respects others' rights and serves the broader goal of collective advancement.

The ability of artificial intelligence technologies to make decisions and act relatively autonomously and to interfere directly or indirectly, positively or negatively, with the activities of human beings raises delicate ethical and deontological questions. Indeed, in certain sectors, such as when AI systems are used by professionals such as doctors, lawyers, notaries, journalists, architects, this aspect probably becomes the most central and must necessarily be reconciled with the ethical principles specific to the various professional categories.

Let's imagine the case of the journalist who uses ChatGPT to write a news article, but does not declare it to avoid his work being belittled. On the one hand, it is not respecting OpenAI's guidelines, which instead require always reporting if the content is the result of artificial intelligence; on the other hand, it exposes itself to the risk of similarity of content, that is, of passing off as its own and original a content that OpenAI has instead provided almost identical to other users.

Another hypothetical example: the doctor who, having to write many drug prescriptions for his patients, decides to get help from an artificial intelligence system and in doing so communicates to the company supplying the system a series of very sensitive personal data (as they are linked to the state of health) without any guarantees of confidentiality; moreover, in doing so, he violates not only the rules on privacy but also those on professional confidentiality.

However, we also have an example that really happened and that concerns the world of photography and therefore even closer to the central themes of this book: the story of the German photographer Boris Eldagsen and his work entitled "PSEUDOMNESIA | The Electrician". Eldagsen created his work not with a photographic process but with Stable Diffusion, a generative artificial intelligence software specialized in hyper-realistic images; and he submitted it to an important photography competition organized by Sony (the Sony World Photography Awards) without specifying the nature of that image. The work was awarded for the "creative open" category, which traditionally includes images that are also retouched, reworked, the result of composition and created with any type of device, but does not say anything explicit about images produced with AI systems. However, the author refused to collect the award and instead raised a question of intellectual honesty and ethics, precisely. In his opinion, his should have been seen more as a provocation and as an opportunity to begin to seriously address the topic of certain new forms of creativity, which cannot always be assimilated to pre-existing ones.

> «I applied as a cheeky monkey, to find out, if the competitions are prepared for AI images to enter. They are not. We, the photo world, need an open discussion. A discussion about what we want to consider photog-

> raphy and what not. Is the umbrella of photography large enough to invite AI images to enter – or would this be a mistake? With my refusal of the award I hope to speed up this debate.»[42]

Eldagsen could have legitimately accepted the award; technically, he hadn't violated the competition rules, and no other legal concerns existed (he held the copyright to the work, and since the depicted subjects were fictional, no image rights issues arose). His hesitation stemmed purely from ethical considerations.

Ethics often provides the most effective framework for addressing the misuse of artificial intelligence; law alone cannot always establish appropriate boundaries. In general, generative artificial intelligence systems are able to create content (images, videos, texts and sounds) that imitate reality sometimes in a perfect and difficult to distinguish way. They can therefore be easily used to create falsifications and manipulations of information and documents, causing the phenomenon of fake news and deep fakes to grow out of all proportion and leading to dangerous cases of manipulation of public opinion or even legal proceedings. In this sense, the use of these systems raises questions about the responsibility of developers and especially of users, who, in the absence of specific legal provisions, will have to find a way to self-regulate by defining rules and guidelines for the correct and "healthy" use of these technologies. In addition, generative AI systems may create content that presents stereotypes and prejudices (for example, racist or sexist images), depending on the

42 Source: https://www.instagram.com/p/Cq_XiGJIQiC/.

content they were trained on and the cultural context in which such training took place. This means that these systems could contribute to amplifying and reinforcing discrimination and inequalities already present in society, triggering a vicious circle of self-perpetuating biases.

On the topic of an ethical approach to the use of AI, the European Parliament has approved a specific resolution, specifically entitled "European Parliament resolution of 20 October 2020 with recommendations to the Commission on a framework of ethical aspects of artificial intelligence, robotics and related technologies"[43]. This document seeks to give a more defined form to the following topics: key concepts of human-centric AI and anthropogenic AI; risk assessment in the use of AI systems; identification of safety, transparency and liability features for AI systems; addressing issues of bias and discrimination, social responsibility and gender balance; environmental sustainability; privacy and biometric recognition; good governance in relation to the development, deployment and use of artificial intelligence, consumer rights in the internal market; employment, workers' rights, digital skills and the workplace; impact of artificial intelligence in education, media, youth, research, sport and the cultural and creative sectors; establishment of national supervisory authorities and their coordination at European level; creation of a European ethical compliance certification.

43 The full text is available at https://www.europarl.europa.eu/doceo/document/TA-9-2020-0275_EN.html.

Chapter 2 – Artificial intelligence and intellectual property: the applicable principles

1. Exclusive rights over artificial intelligence systems and their models

These paragraphs focus on the creation of artificial intelligence systems and the intellectual property rights that emerge for companies operating in this rapidly growing field.

An artificial intelligence system is a complex work consisting of various components, the main one being undoubtedly the software component along with the database used to train the system and the graphical user interface. However, there is also a component that we can call a "model", which is the concept on which the system is based and which enables it to extract new meaning, and, in the case of generative AI, to create new works from what the system itself has "learned"[1].

---

1 These paragraphs partially resume the contents of the article Simone Aliprandi, *La proprietà intellettuale sui modelli di previsione e di profilazione*, in *Ragion pratica*, 2-2021, December ("*Governare l'intelligenza artificiale*", edited by Federico Cabitza, Andrea Rossetti and Susanna Pozzolo).

1.1 Model in what sense

Before proceeding to the more strictly legal discussion, it is important to define what we mean by "model", with particular reference to prediction and profiling models; a phenomenon that is more entrenched and less new than models for creating works (indeed, think of models for weather forecasting or models for profiling consumer habits).

We can generically say that a model is an abstraction, a theoretical and synthetic representation of a reality or phenomenon, which allows and facilitates its study, enabling generalization, didactically exemplifying, making comparisons, formulating hypotheses, and reproducing the behavior of the reality or phenomenon itself.

However, as Thomas Weise points out, models inherently involve some degree of approximation and represent a simplification and idealization of the real world. Weise writes:

> «A model is an abstraction or approximation of a system that allows us to reason and to deduce properties of the system. Models are often simplifications or idealization of real-world issues. They are defined by leaving [out] facts that probably have only minor impact on the conclusions drawn from them.»[2]

Francesco Battaglia, speaking more specifically about the field of statistics, also distinguishes between interpretive and representative models, explaining that:

> «The term «representative» as applied to models [...] is used in contrast to «interpretive» and indicates the

2 Thomas Weise, *Global Optimization Algorithms – Theory and Application*, 3rd edition, p. 107.

absence of explicit assumptions about causal links between phenomena, or other constraints related to a priori knowledge or theories specific to substantive sciences. In other words, if the model has the task of schematizing in mathematical-probabilistic terms the known features [...] of the phenomenon being studied, one speaks of an interpretive model. [...] A representative model, on the other hand, is constructed from data alone, trying to minimize the assumptions made about the behavior of the phenomenon and thus starting from a sufficiently flexible class of possible models, and choosing the one that ensures, according to criteria to be specified, the best representation of the series.»[3]

While models can also be analog (such as wind tunnels for testing vehicle aerodynamics), this abstraction is primarily expressed in quantitative and numerical form. The model typically takes shape as a mathematical expression that can be applied to a set of input data, producing an output that represents the formulated hypothesis or prognosis generated by the model.

Thanks to models, it is therefore possible to hypothesize from a probabilistic point of view future scenarios and, in a certain sense, predict events of nature (as in the classic example of meteorological and epidemiological forecasts), possible evolutions of the economic and social framework, or even behaviors of human beings both understood as groups (see the case of market studies) and understood as individuals (as in the case of profiling done by web platforms); or even assessing the level of risk and danger in certain scenarios and under certain condi-

3 Francesco Battaglia, *Metodi di previsione statistica*, Springer, 2010, p. 187-188.

tions (so-called risk assessment); and finally, a development in recent years, it is possible to create works of ingenuity through simple textual input.

Thus, models nowadays become a particular type of intellectual creation that is extremely strategic. And as such, the question arises whether and in what terms they are subject to protection by industrial and intellectual property law.

1.2. What kind of work is the model?

Perhaps for the sake of simplification, the concept of a model is often equated with that of an algorithm, a procedure expressed as a mathematical formula that solves problems through a finite and determined number of steps. A model does not necessarily take the form of an algorithm; however, models often do because they find their widest application in computer science (as we will see in the following paragraphs).

The attempted assimilation of the concept of model to the concept of algorithm inevitably leads us to wonder about another possible assimilation: that with software, or – according to the classical diction used by our legislator – with computer programs. A mathematical model is not necessarily expressed in the form of computer code; it can be conceived, represented, and extrinsicated in the form of a simple mathematical expression, or of a flowchart, or of an explanatory text of the procedure to be followed in applying the model. It often happens that it is developed by mathematicians, physicists, chemists, statisticians, and economists who have no real technical computer skills, and then it is the task of programmers to transform the theoretical model into software, that is, into lines of code in a specific programming language and with a specific syntax and architecture.

However, although the model is ontologically independent of its expression in software form, it cannot be denied that in recent decades, with the transition to digital technologies, models find their concrete utility and application precisely when expressed in software form. There is a thriving market of installable software and online software-as-a-service platforms that allow modeling in the economic domain, in the statistical domain, in the meteorological domain, in the geophysical and seismic domains; by subscribing to user licenses or terms of service and by paying the corresponding fee/subscription, users obtain the possibility of using an integrated product that contains both the software and the modeling component, in an essentially inseparable way. In many cases the databases that can be used to provide input to the software that implements the model are also offered in the package; and often the databases are also designed and structured so that they are difficult to separate from the software, or at least so that they function only when linked to that specific software.

Having explored these assimilation hypotheses without any being fully applicable, we come to the conclusion that the model is a type of intellectual work that we might call complex, denoting characteristics typical of various categories of works and therefore can access different types of protections as appropriate and sometimes cumulatively.

In particular, building on the points made in the previous paragraph, although theoretically the model is an intellectual work that can also be expressed in forms other than software, de facto we almost always find it expressed in a complex form that contains typical elements of different categories of intellectual works: in particular the more purely theoretical-mathematical part, the computational part with the software architecture and source code, and the database part with the datasets needed for modeling calculations already loaded and embedded in the software package.

Based on this characterization as a complex work, we will proceed in the following paragraphs to examine the intellectual property rights that apply to model protection.

1.3. Exclusive rights over the software component

Based on this framing as a complex work, we will proceed in the next paragraphs with a survey of the intellectual property rights that come into play in the protection of mathematical models.

The software component of the model, if developed with sufficiently original source code, is undoubtedly protected by copyright under Directive 91/250/EEC, which precisely introduced software protection into European supranational law. Article 1 of the directive (related to the object of protection) specifies that "computer programs, in any form expressed as long as they are original as the result of the author's intellectual creation" are protected, and that the term "program" should also be understood to include preparatory material for the design of the program itself; that is, flowcharts, schematics, mathematical expressions, drafts of code and all material from which the architecture of the program can be deduced and from which the creative choices of the developer can be grasped. In return, the directive itself emphasizes that:

> «Ideas and principles which underlie any element of a computer program, including those which underlie its interfaces, are not protected by copyright under this Directive.»

In other words, it is not so much the functionality of a piece of software that is copyrighted, but the architecture of the source code and its syntax. And this complements the thoughts made in paragraph 1.1, confirming that the model achieves more concrete and effective protection when it is expressed in the form of software and does not remain at a level of mere theoretical-mathematical enunciation.

Returning to the text of the directive, in Article 4 we find instead the activities reserved for software authors, which specifically are:

- the permanent or temporary reproduction of a computer program by any means and in any form, in part or in whole. Insofar as loading, displaying, running, transmission or storage of the computer program necessitate such reproduction, such acts shall be subject to authorization by the rightholder;
- the translation, adaptation, arrangement and any other alteration of a computer program and the reproduction of the results thereof, without prejudice to the rights of the person who alters the program;
- any form of distribution to the public, including the rental, of the original computer program or of copies thereof. The first sale in the Community of a copy of a program by the rightholder or with his

> consent shall exhaust the distribution right within the Community of that copy, with the exception of the right to control further rental of the program or a copy thereof.

In other words, these are the rights that the European legal system reserves exclusively for developers or their successors in title, and thus allow commercial exploitation of the software work (through the classic system of user licenses) creating a system of scarcity of the intellectual asset and control by its "owner".

To this, however, must be added the possibility offered by some jurisdictions (mainly in the U.S., but – as we have explained – also in the EU under certain conditions) to file a patent for invention on the algorithms that govern the operation of the system. And in some cases, one must also consider the tendency on the part of software producers to keep the architecture and source code of the work secret and even to include cryptographic and automated systems for rights enforcement (so-called Digital Rights Management or DRM); although – it must be admitted – a good part of the AI systems that are in common use were born with an open source philosophy and therefore there is enough transparency about how they were designed. This scenario accomplishes what is known in the jargon as an accumulation of protections (copyright + patent + trade secret + DRM) and makes software one of the creations covered by greater protections.

1.4. Exclusive rights over the database?

Some software systems are integrated with a database or come bundled with a data component that the software retrieves to provide services to the user. A classic example is a GPS navigation system, which requires complete and up-to-date georeferenced data to function properly, in addition to the navigation software and its graphical user interface.

European law establishes a specific protection regime for databases, which grants two different rights based on whether the database is creative (with data organized according to original criteria) or non-creative and merely compilative (with data arranged following standard or functional criteria). For non-creative databases, a specific right called the "sui generis right of the database maker", established by Directive 96/9/EC in 1996, applies; a right that covers the activities of extraction and reuse of substantial parts of the database. On the other hand, in the case of a database with a creative character, in addition to the sui generis right, a copyright in the more classical sense also applies, thus a right that covers the activities of reproduction, reworking and distribution of the database.

This is one of the most complex areas of intellectual property law, worth understanding at least in its fundamental aspects, particularly given its significant impact on generative artificial intelligence. However, this is not the place to go to a maximum level of detail; for those interested I refer to my other various writings and video lectures.

We can say that the sui generis right constitutes an autonomous legal category, which cannot be assimilated to either copyright or related rights. It is attributed to the person who has made a significant investment in creating a database, referred to as a "maker" or "producer", a figure conceptually distinct from that of the author. A peculiarity of this protection lies in the fact that it does not require the requirement of creative character. In fact, databases are often primarily compilative in nature, deriving their value from the comprehensiveness of collected data and the logic of their organizational structure.

Also particularly relevant to understanding this form of protection are the ways in which databases are used and disseminated. The main risk to which they are exposed is not so much full reproduction as unauthorized extraction and reuse of significant portions of their contents. The sui generis right specifically addresses this threat by protecting the maker against unauthorized extraction and reuse of substantial portions of the database.

Interestingly, sui generis protection also extends to databases containing elements or works not themselves protected by copyright and therefore in the public domain (such as mathematical formulas or texts of judgments). Despite the free usability of the individual contents, the extraction of substantial parts of the database still constitutes a violation of the sui generis right.

It should also be pointed out that the 1996 directive's definition of a database is broad enough to include websites, blogs and social platforms, since all of these rely on underlying databases.

It's worth noting that this section's title deliberately ends with a question mark. Indeed, it is controversial whether it makes sense to speak of a database right in the context of generative artificial intelligence systems, since on closer inspection they do not expose a database in the proper sense, but simply are trained with databases from which they derive mathematical models and the information necessary for their operation.

1.5. Exclusive rights over the "concept". The hypothesis of patenting the model

Finally, beyond the protection reserved for the software component and the database component that go to make up such a complex work, it's also worth examining whether copyright protection can extend to the concept behind the data model and organization—specifically, the overall architecture that enables the various components to function cohesively and effectively together.

In other words, the whole is more than the mere sum of its components; and the choice of how to organize these components and how to make them interact with each other (precisely the overall architecture of the work) is undoubtedly a creative intellectual activity that is therefore eligible for authorial protection.

More importantly, as previously explained, the concept behind the model is typically equated with an algorithm and is almost always expressed in the form of computer code; therefore, it could fall under the definition of "computer implemented inventions" and thus also be the subject of an invention patent.

Whether algorithms themselves can be protected remains a widely debated and unresolved issue, with the U.S. and EU legal systems taking distinctly different approaches. This is not the place to unravel it, but suffice it to say that in the European Union the principle (established in the historic 2006 vote) of non-patentability of software and mere algorithms, remains valid. Nevertheless, information technology companies still manage to obtain patent registrations from the European Patent Office by exploiting the elasticity of the system and making them fall into the category of "computer implemented inventions". In essence, they craft their patent applications to argue that their invention isn't purely software but rather a more complex system in which software is only one component—even when it's often the primary component.

The recently updated Examination Guidelines of the European Patent Office (EPO) refer us to the aforementioned Article 52 of the Munich Convention on the European Patent and the explicit exclusions therein. In paragraph 3.3.2[4] entitled precisely "Simulation, design or modelling" first of all, it is made clear that models are in their own right a subcategory of mathematical methods and should therefore fall under the general principle that excludes their patentability. However, shortly thereafter it is clarified that: «the methods considered in this section, however, are at least partially implemented by means of computers so that the claimed subject matter as a whole is not excluded from patentability.» A series of directions and use cases then follow in order to be able to assess under what terms simulation and modeling methods can produce a technical result and thus be patentable subject matter.

Finally, recall that although the approaches of the U.S. and EU legal systems differ on the issue of soft-

4 Full text is available at https://www.epo.org/law-practice/legal-texts/html/guidelines/e/g_ii_3_3_2.htm.

ware patents, it is on the American continent that a large part of AI systems are developed.

2. The exclusive rights affected by the AI systems training activity

The following sections provide a comprehensive overview of all rights potentially affected by AI training activities. This allows us to get a clear picture of the interests that come into play and, more importantly, which parties can make claims (and civil lawsuits) against AI companies.

2.1. Primarily, the rights of authors

When discussing copyright, it may seem self-evident that authors' rights are the primary consideration. The author of a creative work, by the mere fact of having created it, has a number of rights, which are the rights of: publication; reproduction; transcription; public performance, representation or recitation; communication to the public, i.e., dissemination by means of remote broadcasting (telephone, broadcasting, television, and similar means, including satellite, cable, and the internet itself), including making it available to the public in such a way that each person can have access to it at the place and time individually chosen (so-called on-demand fruitions); distribution; translation and/or processing; rental and lending.

These rights govern the use and economic exploitation of creative works, allowing authors to control how their works are used and to receive appropriate compensation. The holders of these rights may be the authors directly or their successors in title, such as a publishing house or agency that has acquired the rights by contract, or a collective management and brokerage association to which the authors have delegated protection, or the heirs in the event of the death of the authors. These parties are thus the ones who are entitled to authorize the use of their works for training purposes (when precisely it does not fall under fair use or a case of exception to the right) and to charge a corresponding fee.

Beyond these economic rights, many jurisdictions also recognize authors' moral rights. These are rights that concern more than anything the moral and reputational bond between the author and their work and concern aspects such as the right to be recognized as the author of the work or in any case the right to claim paternity of the work; the right to the integrity of the work, or more properly, the right to oppose any deformation, mutilation or other modification that could be prejudicial to their honor or reputation; the right to withdraw the work from commerce for serious moral reasons (emergent after publication).

These rights are strictly personal and as such are also inalienable. It means that even if the author wants to, he or she cannot "get rid" of them completely and cannot dispose of them through licenses, releases and assignment contracts.

The right to claim authorship is frequently confused with the "Attribution" requirement found in Creative Commons and other open licenses. In reality, the Attribution of CCs is a contractual clause that "overlaps" with the moral right and specifies how the author wishes to be referred to. It follows that anyone who uses a Creative Commons-licensed work without citing the author as indicated in the work itself is committing a double violation: violation of the moral right and violation of the "Attribution" contractual clause included in the license.

An issue that is intertwined with the issue of moral rights in copyright is that of maintaining so-called CMI (short for Copyright Management Information), which is the rights ownership information that under U.S. law can only be removed under certain conditions or with the consent of the rights holder. This information often takes the form of "machine readable" metadata and thus is collected in the massive scraping activities of data from the web; however, it is not always easy to maintain it in every activity of reuse and republication of works. Even in jurisdictions where the concept of moral rights is less felt and less central, such as the United States, there are very specific rules prohibiting the removal or concealment of this information. As we shall see later, this issue has also taken on new centrality with the advent of generative artificial intelligence.

2.2. There are also related rights (or neighbouring rights)

The scope of copyright law extends beyond authors in the strict sense to include various other contributors who participate in creating works without having an authorial role: think of figures such as record producers, film producers, actors, singers and instrumentalists. The law reserves to these individuals autonomous rights of protection over their contributions: they are called related rights (or neighbouring rights) and they behave in a substantially similar way to copyrights. Like copyright, these rights enable holders to control how works are used and to receive compensation for such uses. They can also be assigned and subsequently managed by other parties.

Although they are "related" to the exploitation of authors' rights in the strict sense, they often have greater economic weight and their holders possess greater bargaining power than authors. For example, in the sphere of dance and pop music, it frequently happens that songwriters remain in the background compared to the producer, who then becomes the party that actually decides the fate of the songs and thus gets the highest remuneration. Similarly, famous Hollywood actors often become the most visible and highest-paid contributors to a film, overshadowing screenwriters and even directors.

Therefore, it must be kept in mind that when artificial intelligence systems are trained with works that also involve these subjects, due consideration must also be given to the rights of these subjects.

2.3 But above all, there is the sui generis right

We have already explained in the previous paragraphs what the sui generis right to databases is and how it works. We have also explained that those who make AI systems often also make the database part to feed the model and therefore have a sui generis right to that component as well. However, we have to consider that if the training activity is done instead by extracting and reusing data from databases of third parties, then there is a problem of respecting the sui generis right of all those parties.

As a result, in the context of European legislation, sui generis right often becomes the main constraint to be met by those implementing AI systems. It is therefore no coincidence that the European regulation found it necessary to introduce a specific exception for “text and data mining”. This exception, which deserves a separate discussion, operates precisely within the scope of sui generis right, limiting its scope to certain conditions.

The presence of such an exclusive right in the European Union and its absence in the United States adds another layer of complexity to the legal framing of artificial intelligence systems training, creating a significantly differentiated regulatory landscape between the two sides of the Atlantic.

2.4. Some reflections on image rights

The so-called “image rights”, i.e., rights to the image of a person who is recognizable within a photographic, videographic or even pictorial work, deserve a mention.

The key peculiarity lies in the fact that image rights can also involve ordinary people and not necessarily professionals in the creative and entertainment world. Indeed, there is a profound difference between the famous sportsman who knowingly grants his image for an advertising campaign and the private citizen photographed during a labor demonstration. Both hold rights to their own image; however, the athlete willingly shares their image for compensation, while the private citizen often finds their image distributed without prior knowledge or explicit consent.

In the case of private citizens, it is necessary to consider that the right of image is qualified by the legal system as a right of the person and, as such, enjoys particularly incisive protection, enriched also with constraints to protect the honor and reputation of the person portrayed (similarly to the moral rights of copyright, previously discussed). Analyzing the text of Articles 96 and 97, we see that initially a general principle is established that the person portrayed has the right to authorize or prohibit the exploitation of their image; subsequently, some specific cases are outlined in which such explicit consent is not necessary.

Frequently, moreover, the image is disseminated for news or otherwise information needs, and in such circumstances an additional normative layer represented by information law and journalistic ethics comes into play. These constraints become even more stringent when the image involves minor subjects, for whom protection is reinforced by multiple normative sources.

The complexity does not end there. Given that an image of a natural person also falls under the definition of personal data provided by the European GDPR (General Data Protection Regulation), it is also necessary to consider the constraints arising from this legislation. These constraints overlap with those already established in copyright law and often do not harmonize perfectly with the latter, creating a regulatory tangle of complex interpretation.

It follows from this layering of protections that, when it comes to images of private citizens and in particular minors, it is extremely difficult to manage rights according to macrocategories (as the algorithms of web platforms and artificial intelligence systems normally operate). Instead, it becomes necessary to examine each case with the clinical eye of a jurist specialized in information law and personal data protection.

This issue becomes even more significant in the context of training generative AI systems, which automatically process millions of images. The difficulty of assessing the legitimacy of the use of each image on a case-by-case basis poses a significant challenge for the developers of these systems, who have to balance the effectiveness of training with respect for a complex mosaic of individual rights. The risk is in creating systems that unknowingly perpetuate systematic violations of fundamental human rights, with far-reaching ethical and legal implications.

2.5. Some specific cases: the voices of voice actors and the images of famous people

Among the many controversies sparked by generative AI systems, some of the most contentious involve related rights—a legal category growing increasingly important in this rapidly evolving technological landscape.

The case of cloned voices of celebrities represents a particularly emblematic example. Numerous figures from the world of cinema and television have faced situations in which their voices have been replicated and used, without their consent, by generative artificial intelligence systems. The affair involving Scarlett Johansson has become paradigmatic in this regard: the actress became publicly outraged when she discovered that the voice attributed to ChatGPT bore uncanny similarities to her own. The issue was particularly sensitive considering that Johansson had lent her voice to the character of Samantha, an artificial intelligence in Spike Jonze's movie "Her". In that movie, her character was able to establish such a deep emotional relationship with the main character played by Joaquin Phoenix that he fell in love. The irony – her voice being appropriated by a real AI after portraying a fictional one – only intensified the perception that her performance rights had been violated.

The phenomenon has far wider dimensions than a single case. The emergence of platforms such as HeyGen has demonstrated unequivocally that the technology is now sufficiently advanced to challenge the entire movie dubbing industry. These systems can translate and synchronize voices with such precision that, with a few adjustments in post-production, actors could use their original voices for other language versions as well, eliminating the need for professional voice actors. Of course, such use would require that the actors themselves grant explicit permission to the film production to use their voices in such ways. This scenario raises complex questions not only from a legal point of view, but also in terms of the employment impact on an entire professional category that has contributed significantly to the global dissemination of cinematic works.

A similar argument applies to the use of celebrities' images. In Italy, numerous edited music videos where the original performer's face is replaced with that of a famous TV presenter have gone viral. Although this content is mainly made for satirical or recreational purposes, with no direct commercial purposes, from a legal standpoint the TV presenter could legitimately object to the unauthorized use of his image or otherwise demand compensation for such uses. The seemingly innocuous and humorous nature of such content does not eliminate the substantive issue of the right to the image, which remains the prerogative of the person depicted.

These examples illustrate how generative artificial intelligence is redefining the traditional boundaries of related rights, creating novel situations in which legal protection struggles to keep pace with technological evolution. The ease with which voices, faces and artistic performances can be replicated poses significant challenges both for rights holders, who see the possible unauthorized uses of their creations multiplying, and for the regulatory system, which is called upon to balance technological innovation and the protection of individual rights in an ever-changing environment.

2.6. The (all-Italian) problem related to the reproduction of cultural heritage

To complete this overview, we must address another right that can affect the use of AI-generated images: a uniquely Italian legal provision governing the reproduction of cultural heritage. This is the right of reproduction provided for by articles 107 and 108 of the Code of Cultural Heritage and Landscape (Legislative Decree 42/2004), which I and other authors have provocatively defined as a "pseudo-copyright on cultural heritage", since, although it is not a legal institution comparable to either a copyright or a related right, it actually obtains the exact same effect as a restriction on reproductions. Under this provision, anyone seeking to commercially use images of paintings, frescoes, sculptures, bas-reliefs, monuments, or facades of buildings and churches classified as cultural heritage must obtain prior authorization from the institution responsible for the asset and pay a fee calculated according to legally established parameters. And this happens even if the works are largely in the public domain.

This is a principle strongly criticized by various stakeholders and experts, capable of undermining the very concept of public domain and capable of adding constraints on works created many centuries ago when the idea of reproduction and copyright did not even exist. The rationale is to maximize revenue from Italy's invaluable historical and artistic heritage, protect it from exploitative commercial uses, and generate funds for costly conservation and promotion efforts.

I will not go further here and will refer to other writings of mine[5] for a detailed critical analysis of the various problematic aspects of this approach. Here we are more interested in understanding in what terms this "pseudo-copyright" can interfere with the dissemination of images and videos generated with artificial intelligence. One might initially assume that AI-generated images wouldn't qualify as actual photographs of cultural assets, thus avoiding this issue, but it's not that straightforward. In fact, depending on the interpretation given to the rules of the Italian Cultural Heritage Code, this restriction can extend to any reproduction that exploits the image of the cultural asset, including hand-drawn drawings, drawings made with digital tools, up to

5 For instance, see Simone Aliprandi, *The controversial rules for the reproduction of cultural heritage in Italian law*, 17 June 2022, https://medium.com/open-glam/the-controversial-rules-for-the-reproduction-of-cultural-heritage-in-italian-law-9ee552bc49ce.

renderings and virtual graphic representations, such as synthographies made with artificial intelligence (see the examples I created with DALL-E and reported in the image).

Figure 2: experiment in creating images of well-known Italian piece of art, done with DALL-E in 2023 (on the occasion of the first Italian edition of this book).

This "hypertrophic" interpretation of the scope of the right provided for by Articles 107 and 108 of the Cultural Heritage Code, although it may seem absurd to many scholars of the subject, seems to be the one towards which Italian case law is moving. It is sufficient to read the most curious of the precedents currently available in this area: the decision of the Court of Florence[6] obtained in April 2022 by the

6 For a critical comment on the decision, I refer to the article co-written with Carlo Piana titling *Tutela dei beni culturali e lo strano caso di Studi d'arte Cave Michelangelo* and available at

Ministry of Culture against the Carrara company Studi d'Arte Cave Michelangelo (SACM). The company creates marble copies of famous classical sculptures, both using advanced technologies for casting and 3D scanning, and using professional sculptors. In practice, if you're a wealthy art enthusiast wanting a genuine Carrara marble replica of David for your Lake Como villa, or even a marble miniature of the Riace Bronzes for your living room, SACM can fulfill your request. Obviously, to promote this activity, the company has published some images of its products on its website as an example and model. The Florence Court ruled that even photographs of these replicas required museum authorization and fee payment, as they constitute commercial exploitation of the cultural asset's image. Not of the work of art itself, but of its image:

> «Since there is undoubted use of the image of the cultural heritage, it is irrelevant that [...] the issue concerns images of the copy made by the defendant [SACM], especially since this is not perceptible to the public by merely adhering to the statue's gaze being turned to the right instead of the left with different orientation of the sling.»

This is the (quite incredible) conclusion reached by the Italian judge.

As this is a first-instance ruling, we can hope this interpretation will be overturned on appeal. Better yet, someone might challenge the compatibility of Italian legislation with European law regarding public domain works of visual art (Article 14, Directive 2019/790). However, about a year later, in

---

https://aliprandi.blogspot.com/2023/02/beni-culturali-caso-studi-arte-cave-michelangelo-commento-ordinanza.html.

May 2023, the same orientation was confirmed by another provision, again by the Court of Florence and again featuring Michelangelo's David, this time used for the cover of an issue of GQ magazine published by Condé Nast.

Therefore, while waiting (and hoping) for new developments in the regulatory or jurisprudential field, for prudence, in the Italian context and under the Italian law we should be cautious in using images and videos of cultural heritage for commercial purposes, even if created "virtually" with multimedia graphics software or with generative artificial intelligence.

Chapter 3 – The central issue of AI training

1. Just another scraping of the internet

As we have explained (and as is easy to guess), generative artificial intelligence systems need an oceanic amount of data[1], information and content to be trained and to learn ever better to simulate human behavior and human language. The phenomenon of so-called big data intersects precisely this terrain; and it is by no means a coincidence that these new technologies have appeared just after a decade in which the availability of large masses of data has grown exponentially, mostly thanks to the sharing activities of billions of users of social applications and platforms.

The growth trend is exponential and truly staggering. According to Statista.com[2], 90 percent of the world's data has been created in just the past two years. About 328.77 million terabytes, or 0.33 zettabytes, of data are created every day. Monstrous numbers that the human brain struggles to even represent, which are also reflected in the impressive pace at which AI

---

1 For further information, browse the website https://www.data-provenance.org/.

2 See the study *Volume of data/information created, captured, copied, and consumed worldwide from 2010 to 2023, with forecasts from 2024 to 2028*, available at https://www.statista.com/statistics/871513/worldwide-data-created/.

systems are improving forcing us to revisit Moore's Law cycles (or even to foresee the advent of a hyper Moore's law[3]).

There's no use being naive or surprised: the extraction of this "new oil", the massive scraping of information and content from the web, has long been conducted with minimal concern by both public and private entities; and it has been done in defiance of copyright regulations, data protection regulations, and the terms of use of the various websites, invoking more or less legitimate reasons of scientific research, statistical investigation with a social or political background, technological experimentation, even if most of the time it was a less noble profiling of users for commercial purposes.

During the era when "big data" was the buzzword, scraping became almost standard practice, with content owners rarely showing more than mild irritation; because after all, it was a way to gain visibility, to be well indexed, to gather followers. A few years ago, talking to the head of a major research center, to my lawyerly misgivings about their activity of scraping data from major social media for the purpose of doing studies on so-called sentiment analysis, I was told, "we know it shouldn't be done, but everyone does it anyway".

In an interview with Forbes.com[4] in September 2022 by Midjourney founder David Holz, the ques-

---

3 For further information on this topic, see *Narendran Thillaisthanam, Beyond Moore's Law: The Rise of Huang's Law in AI Computing*, 12 January 2025, https://medium.com/@narendrant/beyond-moores-law-the-rise-of-huang-s-law-in-ai-computing-6117b98908d9.

4 See Rob Salkowitz, *Midjourney Founder David Holz On The Impact Of AI On Art, Imagination And The Creative Economy*,

tion "How was the dataset built?" was answered as follows:

> «It's just a big scrape of the Internet. We use the open data sets that are published and train across those. And I'd say that's something that 100% of people do. We weren't picky.»

To the next question, "Did you seek consent from living artists or work still under copyright?" Holz replied:

> «No. There isn't really a way to get a hundred million images and know where they're coming from. It would be cool if images had metadata embedded in them about the copyright owner or something. But that's not a thing; there's not a registry. There's no way to find a picture on the Internet, and then automatically trace it to an owner and then have any way of doing anything to authenticate it.»

The interview came across as a remarkably candid (and perhaps naive) public admission of flagrant disregard for copyright concerns. On the other hand – it is worth repeating here – although many people, due to their ignorance, are truly convinced that if a content is freely accessible on the web, then it is essentially everyone's and no one's (as a kind of *de facto* public domain), the law says otherwise.

Creative work found on the web can only be used lawfully through one of the following avenues: a) verifying that it is in the public domain and therefore free from any exclusive rights; b) verifying that it has been released with an open license (Creative

16 September 2022, https://www.forbes.com/sites/robsalkowitz/2022/09/16/midjourney-founder-david-holz-on-the-impact-of-ai-on-art-imagination-and-the-creative-economy/.

Commons and similar); c) taking advantage of one of the free-use loopholes offered by the legal system (fair use in the U.S. or exceptions to copyright in Europe); d) requesting and obtaining a license from the legitimate rights holders. There is no fifth option. So we need to see whether companies in the field have stayed within these boundaries or forced their hand (as indeed often happens in very innovative fields where the law shows many gray areas).

According to a seductive legal theory (which however still needs to be verified in case law[5]), the activity of mass scraping of web content for the purpose of training artificial intelligence systems would be covered by U.S. fair use doctrine; and, given that a large part of these companies are subject to U.S. law, this would appease them. But of course those on the other side of the fence (authors, publishers, production houses, photography agencies, etc.) are not of this view[6] and have already taken steps to argue their case before the courts, trying to prove instead that that activity is covered by copyright and therefore requires prior permission from the owners. Not only that: in addition to copyright per se, there is a contractual limitation: in fact, almost all websites and social platforms, although freely browsable,

5 See Cala Coffman, *Does the Use of Copyrighted Works to Train AI Qualify as a Fair Use?*, Copyrightalliance.org, 11 April 2023, https://copyrightalliance.org/copyrighted-works-training-ai-fair-use/.

6 Among the studies with this approach, we highlight the white paper *How the pervasive copying of expressive works to train and fuel generative artificial intelligence systems is copyright infringement and not a fair use*, published by News/Media in October 2023, https://www.newsmediaalliance.org/generative-ai-white-paper/.

carry a disclaimer in their terms of use that prohibits massive, automated scraping of content.

Even today, the practice continues with the same "everybody does it" mentality (despite widespread awareness that it's prohibited), but with a difference precisely related to the advent of generative AI systems. Now rights holders perceive more the danger of copyright infringement and competitive activity that returns nothing in either economic or reputational terms, instead bringing wealth and visibility to new players. Here, then, is where lawyers now step in.

Also, to be fair, there would be a need to check on a case-by-case basis how these databases intended for training were made. For example, in the case of image databases we do not always really find the images inside them; often we only find textual descriptors, metadata, with the URL referring to the file present on the original site. Among them, one of the largest and most discussed[7] is LAION-5B (where 5B stands for "5 billions", since it contains more than five billion records), used to train various generative AI systems specializing in images and in particular the better known Stable Diffusion.

In the FAQ[8] on the project's official website, the question "Do LAION datasets respect copyright laws?" is offered this answer:

---

7 In December 2023, some controversy arose as a study by the Stanford Internet Observatory revealed that it indexed images of obvious illicit origin. On this aspect, see David Thiel, *Identifying and Eliminating CSAM in Generative ML Training Data and Models*, Stanford Digital Repository, 2023, https://purl.stanford.edu/kh752sm9123.

8 See https://laion.ai/faq/.

> «LAION datasets are simply indexes to the internet, i.e. lists of URLs to the original images together with the ALT texts found linked to those images. While we downloaded and calculated CLIP embeddings of the pictures to compute similarity scores between pictures and texts, we subsequently discarded all the photos. [...]»

Other databases of the same type have been created using similar methods that should reduce the risk of copyright infringement. For example, Open Images Dataset V7[9] is the database created by Google using images posted on the Flickr platform for photographers under a Creative Commons license or otherwise available in the public domain. Another example is the Multimedia Commons database created by Yahoo! and containing nearly one hundred million images and nearly one million videos posted in Flickr under Creative Commons licenses; it too contains no images but only metadata and external links to the files. Getty Images itself, known for initiating one of the first lawsuits against AI companies, granted licenses that under certain conditions authorized the training of AI systems with its images[10].

In the following image, taken from a screenshot of Open Images Dataset V7, it can be seen that when the original image is for some reason deleted from the original source (Flickr), it is replaced by the words "This image is no longer available in Flickr", while the metadata and descriptors are retained.

9 See https://storage.googleapis.com/openimages/web/index.html.

10 An excellent overview of these databases and how they were built is offered by Paolo Dalprato in his article *Le AI rubano? Sì-no-boh (II°)*, https://www.ai-for-dummies.it/le-ai-rubano-si-no-boh-ii/.

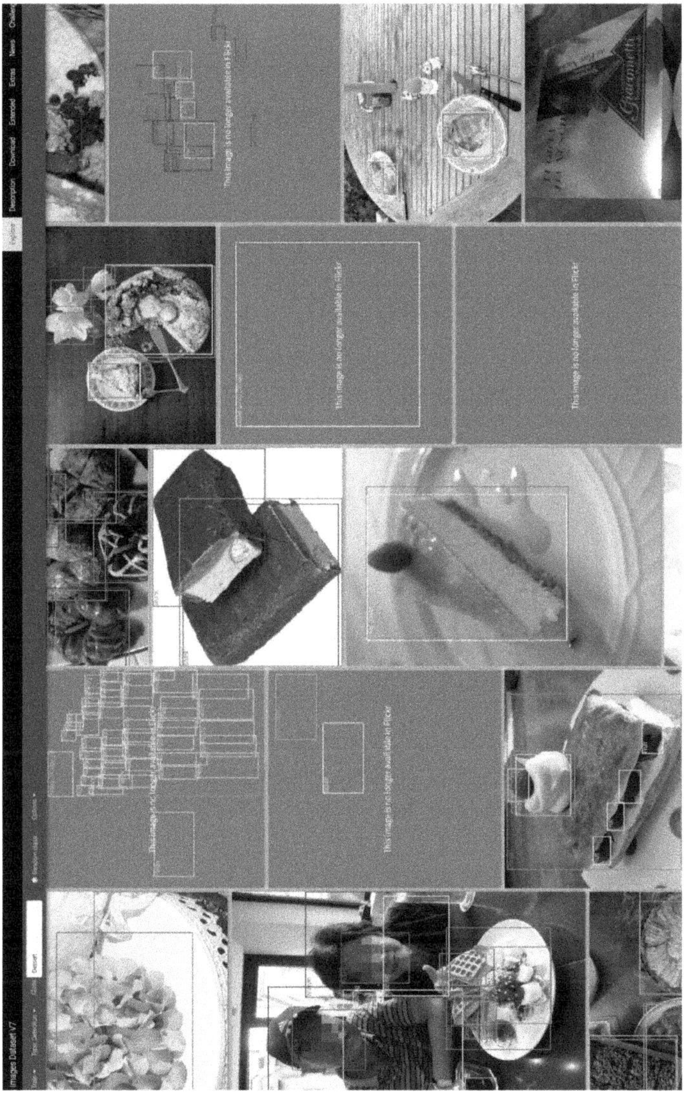

Figure 3: Screenshot of the Open Images Dataset V7 database showing the description criteria and the absence of images remo-

ved from the original source (Flickr).

2. The so-called text and data mining

The extraction of text and data from various documents and creative works (books, photographs, paintings, sculptures, musical compositions, videos and software) is commonly referred to as "text and data mining" or by its acronym, TDM.

Among the data subject to TDM and used for training AI systems may of course be creative works that have not yet fallen into the public domain and thus still protected by a copyright or related right. And even when these are public domain works or mere "raw" unprotected data, there would still be the issue of the sui generis database right, which is precisely a right that covers the activities of extracting and reusing data from databases.

"But big data is freely available on the Internet", many might argue.

The fact that data and content are freely available per se is not enough to argue that scraping from the web (as they say in the jargon) and extracting data from text, images, videos is fully lawful. Except that the expression "freely available" itself is empty of meaning because it should be accompanied by a long series of clarifications: a lot of data and content are on the web against the wishes of their rightful owner (basically because someone who did not ask permission put them there); or they are on the web but accessible only to certain parties or under certain conditions (terms of use, licenses); or they are subject to constraints other than copyright (such as constraints related to privacy, protection of military secrecy, protection of archival and cultural heritage).

Even when AI developers have no intention of creating their own database containing all the operational information to be distributed with the software, machine learning inherently requires the system to acquire data and content, at a minimum as temporary copies. The question of whether temporary copying – which is still a form of copying and reproduction – has copyright implications has occupied the minds of lawyers for many years.

Krista L. Cox, looking at U.S. law that undoubtedly came to deal with these issues early, explains:

> «TDM almost always involves copying, but not all copying amounts to copyright infringement. If TDM merely involves making temporary copies of text and other data for the purposes of analyzing these, and the durable outputs of the computational analysis are merely facts about what is in the literature, then copyright does not apply at all. The reason is that a copyright owner only has the exclusive right to reproduce the article in "copies" and the law defines a "copy" for copyright purposes as one that lasts for a "period of more than a transitory duration". In a case involving copies made by a computer buffer, a federal court of appeals determined that temporary copies that lasted for only 1.2 seconds were transitory and therefore outside the scope of copyright law.»[11]

Although in most jurisdictions there are legal rules that expressly deal with the issue of web-scraping, almost all major social platforms indicate in their

11 Krista L. Cox, *Text and Data Mining and Fair Use in the United States*, FOSTER/Association of Research Libraries, 2015, https://www.arl.org/wp-content/uploads/2015/06/TDM-5JUNE2015.pdf.

terms of use that users are allowed to access content and perhaps even download it for private uses, but massive and systematic scraping is still prohibited. This would be more of a violation of the terms of use and not a violation of a specific legal provision; which is perhaps why this prohibition is mostly ignored or greatly underestimated.

To harmonize the regulatory framework across European countries while introducing greater flexibility for this increasingly common practice, European Directive 2019/790 established specific copyright exceptions for text and data mining—though these primarily benefit research institutions and in any case with various limitations and counter-exceptions; we will have the opportunity to return to this topic later in more detail. We must then keep in mind that much of the AI systems come from the U.S. context so we have to look at their law and not European law. In US law, text and data mining is a form of fair use.

As Matthew Sag points out[12], the U.S. and EU have handled the topic of TDM with very different approaches, and this difference is also reflected by extension on the topic of machine learning and generative artificial intelligence. And the author does not fail to point out that the undoubtedly more flexible U.S. approach creates a more fertile ground for the growth of AI technologies:

> «In the U.S., reproduction in the service of text data mining does not infringe copyright as long as the output of the TDM process itself is not itself infringing.

---

12 Matthew Sag, *Copyright Law's Impact on Machine Intelligence in the United States and the European Union*, in *FIU Law Review*, 2020, https://lawecommons.luc.edu/cgi/viewcontent.cgi?article=1687&context=facpubs.

> The U.S. approach is a triumph for fundamental principles and copyright, and it demonstrates the advantages of the flexible approach of the fair use doctrine. Fundamentally, American courts have understood and respected the most fundamental concept in copyright law, the idea-expression distinction. They have used that principle as the normative content of the fair use doctrine. The basic assumption in copyright is that copyright in the book does not give you copyright in the ideas or the facts embodied within that book. [...] We all know that original expression is required to make something copyrightable in the first place. [...]»

What we explained earlier is thus confirmed: namely, the inherent elasticity and adaptability of common law legal systems, which are based primarily on case law. In fact, Sag's argument continues with the mention of some examples from decisions of American courts that over the years have shaped this specific extension of the fair use doctrine:

> «In the U.S., courts have given life to this principle within the parameters of the fair use doctrine. They have looked at examples like software reverse engineering, plagiarism detection software, book search, meta-analysis of text, and they have seen that although these processes chew up a lot of copyrighted works as inputs, what they spit out the other end is either: (a) not at all copyrightable; or (b) if it is copyrightable, it is just a minor adjunct use like a snippet in a Google search result that is easily justified under traditional transformative use principles. Most importantly, in these examples, there is no expressive substitution for the original work, and that is why these uses have been held, over and over again, to be fair use.»

We should also consider that there will likely be an exponential surge in AI system training activities based not on simple datasets of "raw data" but based on large masses of creative works, such as photographs, paintings, sculptures, music pieces, videos, software, and industrial design projects. Thus, copyright will become an increasingly heartfelt and more complex issue, and it will take a consolidation of case law to bring down the level of legal uncertainty in this area.

Communia Association, an international association that promotes policies aimed at expanding the public domain and free access to culture and knowledge, in its position paper on the topic[13] noted the following:

> «Traditionally, the copyright system has been badly equipped to deal with instances of large numbers of underlying rightholders. Rights clearance for mass digitization projects, for instance, is greatly encumbered by the amount of rightholders and difficulties in obtaining permission from those who either never have or are no longer actively managing their rights. Training ML models from the open internet involves even greater numbers of rightholders. All of this combined with the novelty and rapid development of ML technologies has resulted in significant legal uncertainty. Unsurprisingly, the use of copyrighted works as part of AI training is already subject to legal dispute in the US and UK.»

3. The insidious misunderstanding

13 Policy Paper #15 on using copyrighted works for teaching the machine by Communia Association, https://communia-association.org/2023/04/26/using-copyrighted-works-for-teaching-the-machine-new-policy-paper/.

An easy misconception to fall into – one I initially succumbed to myself – is viewing generative artificial intelligence as a system that, given specific user input, actively searches databases or the Internet for relevant information, instantly processes it, reassembles it creatively, and delivers it as output.

In reality, the mechanism is different. The AI responds not so much by re-pasting things it has in a phantom memory of its own, but by proposing something that is generated instantaneously on the basis of what the system has learned to do and what it thinks will best satisfy the user's request (from a probabilistic perspective). This partially explains the phenomenon known as "hallucinations": when an AI doesn't know an answer, rather than acknowledging this limitation, it often generates a plausible but factually incorrect response.

We can therefore say that if we feed an AI system a large dataset of text, images, videos or other works, it analyzes it not so much by trying to "copy" the various contents, but by trying as much as possible to learn how to create similar things, emulating the human learning system. In the neural network, therefore, copies of the images are not saved, but a statistical projection is made of them, patterns are drawn from them that will then allow the AI to generate credible things, as similar as possible to those that a human being would create if called upon to perform the same task.

Rather than copying in the traditional sense, this appears to be more a process of data extraction and reuse, falling less within the domain of classic copyright and more under the sui generis right of database creators; a particular right to protect databases established by Directive 96/9/EC. Thus, however, we encounter an additional layer of complexity: this right exists only in the EU and finds no equivalent in the U.S., the home of much of AI technology. In essence, U.S. companies can pose fewer concerns than European companies and have higher hopes of being able to leverage fair use. As a result, even in terms of intellectual property, the Old Continent confirms itself as a land not very favourable to the growth of these technologies.

In conclusion, however, I see it quite remote that the user may face copyright infringement challenges for merely using generative AI, when it is done in good faith and in line with the terms of use of the various platforms. The copyright issue, assuming precisely that it can be shown that there is a derivative relationship between the works used for training and the output provided, will concern at most the companies producing the AI systems and the rights holders; and will remain on the level of civil damages.

These systems can hardly be asked to go back, to "unlearn" what they have learned to do; by the way, I do not think this is in anyone's interest, not even the rights holders who could instead profit handsomely in terms of damages and royalties from a monstrously growing industry.

FOCUS

A very common misconception about AI

- It is essential to understand that AI is not something that, following our input, goes looking for various things on the net, re-mixes them and offers them to us as output. It doesn't work like that!

- In reality, behind AI there is a learning process that emulates human learning; and the generation of content is the result of what the AI has learned, not so much of a "remix" of pre-existing elements.

4. The recurring (and wrong) question: do AIs "plagiarize" works?

But then do generative AIs, when they provide their output in response to the prompt entered by the user, not copy the works they "digested" in the training phase? And if they do not copy them, do they nonetheless reproduce substantial creative elements of them such that there was a reworking of a pre-existing work? The question is as decisive as it is complex, because it requires a technical knowledge of how these systems work that is beyond the reach of everyone.

From a legal point of view, perhaps the more correct question to ask is: do the outputs of generative AI systems reproduce creative elements of pre-existing works in a way that exposes the user to the risk of infringing (albeit unknowingly) someone else's copyright and suffering legal consequences? Or also: is there a derivative relationship between the works used for training and the works generated by AI as output?

The answer is the most frustrating (yet most common and truthful) response a legal expert can give: it depends!

It depends first of all on the prompt provided by the user. On the other hand, if I ask a generative AI system to "create a black-and-white syntograph of a sailor passionately kissing a nurse during the celebrations in Time Square for the end of World War II that is very similar to Alfred Eisenstaedt's famous photograph V-J day in Times Square", it is clear that the system will be led to recreate an image very similar to the historic photograph we all know and which is currently still copyrighted (since Eisenstaedt has been dead for less than 70 years).

Let's experiment with Copilot Designer. By providing exactly that prompt, the system responds that the request cannot be fulfilled because it includes wording that could violate the platform's terms of use. Basically, the system noticed that I was trying to do an activity with my prompt that potentially conflicted with copyright and policies established by Microsoft and an alarm bell went off.

Figure 4: Copilot Designer response with a notice of internal policy violation.

We then modify the prompt, removing any explicit reference to the famous photo, but providing specific information about what the image must look like; information, however, that does no more than describe Eisenstaedt's famous photo in detail. The new prompt is as follows:

> «create a black-and-white photograph of a sailor passionately kissing a nurse during celebrations in Time Square for the end of World War II in August 1945. The sailor has a classic plain dark blue sailor uniform, the nurse has a classic all-white nurse outfit. The kiss must be a kind of casquet (as in dancing). The nurse must look a little surprised. In the background there must be other sailors and nurses smilingly watching the scene.»

In this case the system does not inhibit and gives me this image as a result.

Figure 5: First image generated with Copilot Designer.

The image bears striking similarities to Eisenstaedt's photo, including elements I never explicitly mentioned in my prompt, such as the sailor's rightward orientation and the white hat.

We could engage in endless speculation and theorizing, but this wouldn't necessarily bring us closer to understanding what actually occurred. Did Copilot provide me with that result because it "had the famous copyrighted photograph in its stomach" anyway, and did nothing more than resubmit something similar to it to me? Did Copilot provide me with that result simply because it carried out my instructions? Did Copilot provide me with that result because in training anyway it "saw and studied" the famous photograph a lot of times, in various versions and reworkings done by various artists, photographers and designers?

The answer is in my view always in statistics. That is, the artificial intelligence provided the thing that a human designer would most likely think of if given such a prompt. In other words, Copilot has seen that image and similar images inspired by it so many times that it has made it an important reference of its own; on a par with students in a photography or drawing class.

Basically, if we talk about sailors kissing nurses to celebrate the end of a war, from a probabilistic perspective the first connection that comes is to the famous 1945 photo. It is so with the human mind: and it is so with artificial intelligence that precisely seeks to emulate the workings of the human mind.

I then also asked myself another question: would the result be similar even without indicating which war and which historical period we are talking about, without indicating the color of the clothes, without indicating Time Square as the location?

We then do a further experiment by modifying the prompt and making it less specific:

> «create a black-and-white photograph of a sailor passionately kissing a nurse during celebrations for the end of the war. The sailor has a classic sailor uniform, the nurse has a classic nurse outfit. The kiss must be a kind of casquet. The nurse must look a little surprised. In the background there must be many other people watching the scene.»

And here is the image that was provided to me:

Figure 6: Second image generated with Copilot Designer.

The result can be disorienting, but it confirms what I wrote just above. Despite the lesser detail provided in the prompt, the image remains very similar to Eisenstaedt's photo; and indeed, in some respects it is even more similar.

By giving more freedom to the generative algorithm, statistics played an even greater role. Can we really talk about plagiarism in cases like this?

I deliberately leave the question open; but nevertheless I want to conclude my reflection by quoting the words of an American judge who decided a judicial case precisely on the hypothesis of plagiarism by ChatGPT and who will be the subject of a more pointed commentary in the next set of paragraphs:

> «When a user inputs a question into ChatGPT, ChatGPT synthesizes the relevant information in its repository into an answer. Given the quantity of information contained in the repository, the likelihood that ChatGPT would output plagiarized content from one of the Plaintiffs' articles seems remote.»[14]

The plaintiffs of the lawsuit are the U.S. companies Raw Story Media Inc. and AlterNet Media Inc. (owners of online news outlets and producers of news content) and the defendant is OpenAI, held liable for copyright infringement in the training of ChatGPT and the provision of the outputs.

Obviously the judge's words concern only the specific case and must be contextualized to the judicial affair; but they are undoubtedly very emblematic.

5. Do generative AIs copy artists' style (and thus infringe copyright for that)?

Another criticism that is often levelled at generative AI systems is that they copy the styles of particularly iconic and recognizable artists, that they make parasitic imitations without originality and thus violate some sort of "moral right" of authors. Classic examples are prompts such as "edit this photograph of mine and make it look like a Salvador Dalí painting"; or "for this chord sequence, generate a guitar solo as David Gilmour would write it and play it".

---

14 Decision and order by Judge McMahon in the case between Raw Story Media & AlterNet Media (Plaintiffs) vs OpenAI (Defendant), United States District Court – Southern District of New York; 7 November 2024, https://zenodo.org/records/14317998.

This criticism, however, reveals a limited understanding of both the underlying legal principles and the functional mechanics of generative artificial intelligence.

Before claiming copyright infringement based on the imitation of an author's style, one must first determine whether that style actually qualifies for copyright protection. The approaches of various legal systems around the world may differ on this issue, but in general, style itself is not covered by copyright protection because it is too abstract and undefined. Copyright tends to protect the expressive form of works but not the idea behind it (which is instead replicable by anyone), much less the method by which the author arrived at the final result. However, the issue is complex and full of nuances, because in any case the characterization of fictional characters and the concept of a literary, graphic or film work are instead fully subject to copyright protection. Let us try to delve deeper and understand it better.

As Arlo Canella aptly explains,

> «the difficulty of protecting style lies in the fact that it is an «abstract concept» that reflects the artist's personal approach to creation, rather than a not specific tangible element.»

But beyond the question of technical-legal difficulty in protecting something so abstract and undefined, Canella also rightly points out a fundamental question of expediency:

> «before protecting a pure concept or style, we need to think deeply about the impact this choice might have on the freedom of expression of us all. The defense of style remains a complex and nuanced area of law, requiring balance between the protection of individual

> creativity, respect for and artistic feeling of others, and the freedom of inspiration for expression.»

Of the same opinion is Stephen Wolfson, who in an article for the Creativecommons.org[15] website writes:

> «Style is not generally protected by copyright, and that›s a good thing; if one artist were given a monopoly over anime, grunge music, or other styles, that would frustrate copyright's core purpose of supporting creativity. [...] Copyright doesn't protect things like style and genre, because doing so would limit the ways that others can create other works, thereby chilling their ability to express themselves through their works.»

A similar debate, in fact, had already arisen a few years ago, well before the advent of generative artificial intelligence systems, when some applications that allowed images to be modified in the style of famous comics or cartoons began to spread. Particularly well known and used are the web services or mobile apps that, by uploading one's own portrait photo, are able to transform us into a Simpsons character, with the classic "yellow" style that came out of Matt Groening's creative mind and the characteristic setting based on glimpses of Springfield. However, there are many other services that do the same thing for other famous cartoons or comics (Family Guy, South Park, Dragon Ball). Does anyone really think that Matt Groening could make copyright demands of the users of all those services? At most, he could make claims to the providers of those services; but not so much because of the style itself, but because

15 See Stephen Wolfson, *The Complex World of Style, Copyright, and Generative AI*, 23 March 2023, https://creativecommons.org/2023/03/23/the-complex-world-of-style-copyright-and-generative-ai/.

specific creative elements are often replicated, such as wallpapers replicating the Simpsons' house or replicas of certain Simpsons characters. And even in those cases, the use could be considered sufficiently transformative under U.S. fair use.

At the time of closing of this book's writing, the issue of alleged copyright infringement by slavishly imitating the style of some artists is still hotly debated. With the version of the image generator launched by OpenAI in March 2025, many users have ventured into creating "Ghibli-style" images, rekindling doubts about copyright infringement. Studio Ghibli, founded by Hayao Miyazaki, is a major Japanese animated film studio that since the mid-1980s has been distinguished by a particularly recognizable trait (on par with what Matt Groening did a few years later with his yellow characters).

In a statement to the New York Times and published on March 27, 2025[16], Taya Christianson of OpenAI, after stressing the importance of giving ChatGPT users as much creative freedom as possible, reiterated that OpenAI, according to its policies, "continues to prevent generations in the style of individual living artists, but we do permit broader studio styles — which people have used to generate and share some truly delightful and inspired original fan creations". A turn of phrase that, in fact, explains little and seems more like an evasive response; and especially one that purports to leverage a distinction (that between individual artist and production studio) that is not reflected in copyright law.

---

16 Madison Malone Kircher, *People Love Studio Ghibli. But Should They Be Able to Recreate It?*, 27 March 2025, https://www.nytimes.com/2025/03/27/style/ai-chatgpt-studio-ghibli.html.

Commenting on the very news about the massive use of "Studio Ghibli style" by ChatGPT users, Edward Lee, a lawyer who is very precise in commenting on these issues, expressed his opinion as follows[17]:

> «While it's true broader styles (e.g., Cubism and Surrealism) are not copyrightable to one artist, the distinctive style of one artist, such as Saul Steinberg, who illustrated covers for the New Yorker, is a part of their copyrightable expression. Dr. Seuss was another artist who had a very distinctive visual (and literary) style.»

Lee thus seems to lurch toward the protectability of artists' style. In any case, he adds that nevertheless delineating these boundaries well will be one of the most interesting tasks facing judges in the coming years, again deferring the most concrete answers to the coming case law:

> «Granted, litigation will determine the scope of copyright protection for an artist's asserted distinctive style–what the elements of the style are and which are protected by copyright. At some point, a style may be or become too broad because it constitutes a general approach or genre. And, with some types of works, such as musical works, assertions of copyright over a personal style of one musician may be problematic because it may overlap too much with elements that define heavily genre-based types of works (e.g., rap, country, pop music) that all artists use. But, where the intended target of copying is not a general style, but instead one artist's distinctive style, that may raise a question of copyright infringement.»

17 Edward Lee, *Studio Ghibli v. OpenAI: is this the next U.S. copyright lawsuit to drop?*, 28 March 2025, https://chatgptiseatingtheworld.com/2025/03/28/ghibli-studios-v-openai-is-this-next-u-s-copyright-lawsuit-to-drop/.

Finally, Lee concludes by cautioning that, in his view, it is false to say that copyright never protects an artist's style, as "[U.S.] Case law already recognizes that an artist's distinctive style is a part of expression and may fall within copyright protection".

Lee's opinion, although authoritative and well-argued, nevertheless reflects a minority approach and helps us understand how these arguments still carry with them many nuances and gray areas for the law.

6. A new market is born: licenses for training AI systems

The proliferation of generative AI platforms and applications has spawned an entirely new market: training licenses. Rights holders (publishers, record companies, film producers, authors' associations) have already entered into negotiations to assign licenses for training AI systems for a fee. This phenomenon represents a significant turning point in the copyright landscape, as it introduces new economic and legal dynamics.

This market is especially vibrant now that AI system developers have evolved into massive concentrations of capital and economic power, enabling them to afford such licensing fees and settle the various lawsuits that have emerged in recent years regarding training practices. The availability of financial resources on the part of these companies has made it possible to negotiate settlements that, just a few years ago, would have been unthinkable.

Companies involved in this emerging market include tech giants such as Google, Meta, and OpenAI, which have faced a number of copyright lawsuits because of their use of generative artificial intelligence technologies. These companies have trained models by providing them with large amounts of content, often without the consent of rights holders and leveraging fair use. To resolve these disputes, negotiations have been initiated to obtain licenses to allow the legal use of such content.

On the one hand, content creators see these licenses as a new source of revenue; on the other hand, AI companies recognize the importance of access to high-quality data to improve their algorithms. This balance of interests has created a dynamic and evolving marketplace, where negotiations are often complex and require a deep understanding of the legal and commercial implications.

Entities have also sprung up precisely to carry the interests of players in this new field. The Dataset Providers Alliance (DPA)[18], for example, is a trade group formed by seven content licensing vendors that specialize in providing music, images, video and other datasets for training artificial intelligence systems. DPA aims to raise awareness and establish standards to ensure that licensed data is used in a lawful manner.

The future of intellectual property in the age of artificial intelligence will also be shaped by this emerging new contracting practice, and collaboration between

18 On the home page of the official website (https://www.thedpa.ai/) we read: «The DPA brings together a diverse range of AI data licensing providers and intellectual property owners, including those specializing in music, voice, text, video, and images. By establishing a unified voice for dataset providers, the alliance advocates for the interests of rights holders and works to create a sustainable and equitable ecosystem for the licensing of intellectual property content in the AI and ML industries.»

content creators and AI companies will be key to ensuring a balance between technological innovation and copyright compliance.

There is a dark side, however: since we are dealing with contractual dynamics, there is obviously a risk that the rules of the game will be skewed by the strengths of the players involved and that in essence it is only the players with great economic power who can drive the new contracting practice.

Illuminating on this point is the warning issued by Martin Adams in a commentary[19] of the case law case Thomson Reuters vs. ROSS (discussed a little later).

Adams reports that if the judge's arguments gain traction:

> «they could further entrench the dominance of a few large AI companies. Only major players like Microsoft and Meta will be able to afford AI training licenses, consolidating control over the industry. The AI training licensing terms will be determined solely between big AI companies and big content aggregators, without representation of individual authors or public interest. The large content aggregators will get to dictate the terms under which creators must surrender rights to their works for AI training, and the AI companies will dictate how their AI models can be used by the general public.»

Adams also points out the need for legislators to intervene with new regulations to restore a balance:

> «Without meaningful pushback and policy intervention, smaller organizations and individual creators

19 Martin Adams, *Thomson Reuters v. ROSS: the first AI fair use ruling fails to persuade*, 13 February 2025, https://www.authorsalliance.org/2025/02/13/thomson-reuters-v-ross-the-first-ai-fair-use-ruling-fails-to-persuade/.

cannot participate fairly. Let's not rewrite our copyright laws to entrench this power imbalance even further.»

7. Fair use and transformative use: the U.S. approach

Now we arrive at the crux of the issue, which requires a clear understanding of how generative artificial intelligence systems actually operate.

If I enter as a prompt "create a portrait of Queen Elizabeth in the Cubist style as Pablo Picasso would have done it", it is assumed that the AI system to produce something satisfactory has "chewed up" many works by Picasso and other artists who followed his style. Both Picasso and other artists of his "school" tend to still be protected authors because the statutory 70 years after death for passage into the public domain have not yet passed. Doubt about possible copyright infringement is therefore not entirely unfounded.

The user entering the prompt, however, has limited concern about this aspect, since the AI system's developer may have already secured proper licensing for using Picasso's images in training; among other things, the principles of fair use that we recalled in the previous paragraph would come into play. Rather, the user is interested in whether the image obtained as an output is to be considered a kind of derivative work of Picasso's paintings and consequently whether – to put it in simple terms – accountability to Picasso's heirs is also required at the time the decision is made to disseminate the output work.

At this level too, without specific regulations in place, we must fall back on general legal principles concerning derivative works and creative adaptations, again highlighting the divergent approaches between Anglo-American and EU legal frameworks.

In countries where there is a focus on moral rights, one could raise the issue of imitation of a particular style of a specific author; but this is a forced assumption and would require a solid argument in case law.

In addition, there is the aforementioned problem of the sui generis right, which is why a specific and express exception on text and data extraction was necessary. Adding further complexity to the EU legal landscape is an additional potentially conflicting right: the newly established protection for publishers of journalistic content under Article 15 of Directive 2019/790/EU.

For argument's sake, we might set these concerns aside given that most AI systems currently originate from the U.S., requiring us to apply legal frameworks typical of that jurisdiction.

As we have already mentioned, under US law transformative use of protected works is covered by the umbrella of fair use. The USCO website's page devoted to the concept of fair use (itself based on the principles set by the US law makers in Section 107 of the 1976 Copyright Act and case law developed over the decades) defines transformative use very succinctly: "A transformative use adds 'new expression, meaning, or message' to the original work. It's more likely to qualify as fair use than non-transformative copying".

Transformativeness is thus a quality of derivative works that allows them to surpass or recontextualize the original works from which they derive. A characteristic that has become increasingly central with the advent of digital creativity and communication via the Internet (think, for example, of the meme phenomenon); in this world, the transformative characteristic of the later work is often to provide the audience with a previously unavailable benefit that would otherwise remain unavailable. This transformative quality carries significant weight in fair use analyses and can legitimize what might otherwise appear as straightforward copyright infringement[20].

Confirming this principle came an important ruling (Campbell v. Acuff-Rose Music, 510 U.S. 569 (1994), U.S. Supreme Court[21]), which, arguing on one of the four factors posed by Section 107 to determine whether there is fair use, clarified:

> «Under the first of the four § 107 factors, "the purpose and character of the use, including whether such use is of a commercial nature..." the enquiry focuses on whether the new work merely supersedes the objects of the original creation, or whether and to what extent it is "transformative", altering the original with new expression, meaning, or message. The more transformative the new work, the less will be the significance of other factors, like commercialism, that may weigh against a finding of fair use.»

20 For a better understanding, I recommend reading the specific entry "Transformative use" on Wikipedia (https://en.wikipedia.org/wiki/Transformative_use) and the list of concrete examples of transformative use compiled by lawyers Richard Stim and Glen Secor (https://www.nolo.com/legal-encyclopedia/fair-use-what-transformative.html).

21 https://en.wikipedia.org/wiki/Campbell_v._Acuff-Rose_Music,_Inc.

FOCUS

Who owns the rights to AI-generated works?

Cold answer → IT DEPENDS!
But... it depends on what?

It depends on whether there is actually a creative activity by a human author.

- If there is creative activity, the rights belong to the author who created the work using an AI.
- If there is no creative activity, *perhaps* there is no right (and therefore the works would be in the public domain from the beginning).

It depends on what the terms of the AI service you use say.

- AI services (although not all of them) usually assign usage rights to the user..

8. The viewpoint of European law

The European Union has likewise moved to establish preliminary regulations for this emerging field. We'll examine specifically the "text and data mining" exception in Directive 2019/790/EU on Copyright in the Digital Single Market (the CDSM Directive) and Regulation 2024/1689/EU, more widely known as the European Artificial Intelligence Regulation or AI Act[22].

22 More properly it is titled Regulation (EU) 2024/1689 of the European Parliament and of the Council of 13 June 2024 laying down harmonised rules on artificial intelligence and amending Regulations (EC) No 300/2008, (EU) No 167/2013, (EU) No 168/2013, (EU) 2018/858, (EU) 2018/1139 and (EU) 2019/2144 and Directives 2014/90/EU, (EU) 2016/797 and

8.1. The 2019 CDSM directive and the text and data mining exception

As previously noted, Article 4 of the CDSM Directive introduces a specific copyright exception "for reproductions and extractions made from works or other materials to which access is lawfully given for the purpose of "text and data mining", or simply TDM.

We reproduce the text of Article 4 in its four paragraphs in its entirety:

1. Member States shall provide for an exception or limitation to the rights provided for in Article 5(a) and Article 7(1) of Directive 96/9/EC, Article 2 of Directive 2001/29/EC, Article 4(1)(a) and (b) of Directive 2009/24/EC and Article 15(1) of this Directive for reproductions and extractions of lawfully accessible works and other subject matter for the purposes of text and data mining.
2. Reproductions and extractions made pursuant to paragraph 1 may be retained for as long as is necessary for the purposes of text and data mining.
3. The exception or limitation provided for in paragraph 1 shall apply on condition that the use of works and other subject matter referred to in that paragraph has not been expressly reserved by their rightholders in an appropriate manner, such as machine-readable means in the case of content made publicly available online.
4. This Article shall not affect the application of Article 3 of this Directive.

(EU) 2020/1828 (Artificial Intelligence Act). The full text is available at https://eur-lex.europa.eu/eli/reg/2024/1689/.

Copyright exceptions essentially create safe harbors where creators' usage rights yield to other rights and interests that the legal system prioritizes as more worthy of protection. When an exception is provided then the use of the work can be made without having to obtain permission from the rights holder, obviously staying within the boundaries established by the exception itself.

Whereas Articles 5 and 8 of the directive explain the theoretical and political assumptions that led the EU to introduce the new rules:

> [5] In the fields of research, innovation, education and preservation of cultural heritage, digital technologies permit new types of uses that are not clearly covered by the existing Union rules on exceptions and limitations. [...] Mandatory exceptions or limitations for uses of text and data mining technologies, illustration for teaching in the digital environment and for preservation of cultural heritage should be introduced. [...]

> [8] New technologies enable the automated computational analysis of information in digital form, such as text, sounds, images or data, generally known as text and data mining. Text and data mining makes the processing of large amounts of information with a view to gaining new knowledge and discovering new trends possible. Text and data mining technologies are prevalent across the digital economy; however, there is widespread acknowledgment that text and data mining can, in particular, benefit the research community and, in so doing, support innovation. Such technologies benefit universities and other research organisations, as well as cultural heritage institutions since they could also carry out research in the context of their main activities. However, in the Union, such organisations

> and institutions are confronted with legal uncertainty as to the extent to which they can perform text and data mining of content. In certain instances, text and data mining can involve acts protected by copyright, by the sui generis database right or by both [...]. Where no exception or limitation applies, an authorisation to undertake such acts is required from rightholders.

The primary purpose of these new regulations is to reduce legal uncertainty about permissible activities while simultaneously fostering conditions conducive to innovation and research.

The exception's scope appears quite limited, however, both because it primarily applies to scientific research in academic and nonprofit contexts, and because, despite offering some flexibility, it allows rights holders to effectively neutralize the exception by explicitly reserving rights over text and data extraction (Paragraph 3 of Article 4).

8.2. The 2020 Resolution and the AI Act

Shortly after the directive came into force, the European Union also more specifically addressed the issue of intellectual property on works created with AI systems through a resolution of the European Parliament: the 20 October 2020 on intellectual property rights for the development of artificial intelligence technologies[23]. This document was the starting point for the institutional debates on the delicate relationship between intellectual property law and generative artificial intelligence systems that became

23 The full text is available at https://www.europarl.europa.eu/doceo/document/TA-9-2020-0277_EN.html.

particularly heated after the fateful fall of 2022 with the public release of ChatGPT and various image generation platforms.

This continued until the European Regulation on Artificial Intelligence was drafted and approved. Notably, the initial draft published in April 2021 made no mention whatsoever of intellectual property issues[24]. In general, it was a regulatory text aimed at classifying AI systems according to the level of risk and establishing the related limits and responsibilities. It was not until 2023, due to the impetus of the debate on the topic of new forms of creativity and AI training with protected works, that it was considered to introduce some copyright rules; leading to the final text that was approved on May 13, 2024 and entered into force on August 1 of the same year.

Even in the final text, copyright concerns remain peripheral compared to the regulation's central focus on risk management and associated responsibilities. In fact, one only has to do a text search to notice that the term "copyright" appears only once in the articles of the regulation (in Article 53); while the term "intellectual property" appears only four times (in Articles 26, 52, 53, and 78); yet none of these rules are specifically devoted to the topic.

The AI Act generally approaches intellectual property concerns through a transparency framework, requiring AI system providers and deployers to

24 The same thing goes for the "White Paper on Artificial Intelligence – A European approach to excellence and trust" published by the European Commission on 19 February 2020 in which not even the words "copyright" or "intellectual property" appear. See full text at https://commission.europa.eu/system/files/2020-02/commission-white-paper-artificial-intelligence-feb2020_en.pdf.

disclose when content is artificially generated and, crucially, to reveal which datasets were used to train their models.

Specifically, Article 50 (titled "Transparency obligations for providers and deployers of certain AI systems") states in paragraph 2:

> «Providers of AI systems, including general-purpose AI systems, generating synthetic audio, image, video or text content, shall ensure that the outputs of the AI system are marked in a machine-readable format and detectable as artificially generated or manipulated.»

But the most central provision for the delicate subject of training is Article 53 ("Obligations for providers of general-purpose AI models"), which in turn refers to Annex XI of the regulation. Paragraph 1 of Article 53 reads:

> «Providers of general-purpose AI models shall:
>
> (a) draw up and keep up-to-date the technical documentation of the model, including its training and testing process and the results of its evaluation, which shall contain, at a minimum, the information set out in Annex XI for the purpose of providing it, upon request, to the AI Office and the national competent authorities;
>
> [...]
>
> (c) put in place a policy to comply with Union law on copyright and related rights, and in particular to identify and comply with, including through state-of-the-art technologies, a reservation of rights expressed pursuant to Article 4(3) of Directive (EU) 2019/790;
>
> (d) draw up and make publicly available a sufficiently detailed summary about the content used for train-

> ing of the general-purpose AI model, according to a template provided by the AI Office.»

Currently, it is premature to evaluate the effectiveness of this regulatory approach, and particularly unclear how these obligations will be enforced in practice.

Chapter 4 – The most interesting copyright infringement lawsuits in AI training

1. Introduction

When dealing with cutting-edge issues like those discussed in these pages (particularly AI training), examining relevant case law and explaining the nature of these disputes provides valuable insight. This is especially relevant considering that many companies in the AI sector are based in common law countries (such as the United States) where a ruling by a court, in addition to exposing the valuable legal argument on which the judges based their decision, creates the legitimate expectation that the other judges will also follow the same orientation, thus consolidating the applied jurisprudential principles.

Often, however, we hear about the initiation of legal proceedings but never get to see a formal ruling, despite the fact that the case touches on really delicate and intriguing legal knots and thus is crucial for framing many similar cases. This occurs because, in civil cases, the parties frequently reach settlements during proceedings, with the terms almost always subject to confidentiality agreements.

In all those cases all we can do is to report what emerges from the court documents submitted by the parties and any interlocutory orders of the judges.

These documents often contain valuable insights and serve as a foundation for legal analysis; however, they cannot establish legal precedent because they lack a final judicial decision.

2. Andersen + McKernan + Ortiz vs. Stability AI Ltd. + Midjourney Inc. + DeviantArt, Inc.

The first lawsuit[1] was brought by a group of three graphic and figurative artists (Sarah Andersen, Kelly McKernan, Karla Ortiz) who, represented by attorneys Matthew Butterick and Joseph Saveri, filed a class-action lawsuit in the United States District Court for the Northern District of California (San Francisco). The defendants are the companies behind two of the leading generative artificial intelligence platforms: Stable Diffusion (with companies Stability AI Ltd. and Stability AI Inc.) and Midjourney (with company Midjourney Inc.); we also find Deviantart.com (with company DeviantArt Inc.), a website that provides a platform for storing and sharing graphic works. In parallel, Butterick and Saveri also sued Microsoft, GitHub, and OpenAI in another similar judgment revolving around the CoPilot AI programming model.

From a corporate communications perspective, Midjourney Inc.'s management clearly failed to handle these matters with appropriate sensitivity and due diligence. As we have already recounted in the

1 All documents related to this court case are available at https://www.courtlistener.com/docket/66732129/andersen-v-stability-ai-ltd/.

preceding paragraphs, Midjourney founder David Holz made legally self-defeating statements, openly declaring in interviews and public announcements that he had done massive scraping of images from the web "without being picky" and without much concern for copyright compliance and terms of use of the various sites.

These statements sounded like a kind of public admission of blatant carelessness in handling the copyright issue, perpetuating the common misconception that everything on the Internet is exempt from copyright concerns because it is de facto in the public domain; this on the one hand sparked speculation among commentators, and on the other offered a good starting point for lawyers who wanted to "open hostilities".

The plaintiffs therefore acted to obtain damages attributable in their opinion to Stable Diffusion, Midjourney, and DeviantArt and to seek an injunction to prevent further damages. As Aaron Moss aptly points out, the true motivation behind this legal action is captured in the opening statement of the complaint, which declares that "the plaintiffs seek to end this blatant and egregious violation of their rights before their professions are eliminated by a computer program powered entirely by their hard work".

The complaint filed by attorneys Butterick and Saveri has been criticized by experts from the outset for containing several technical inaccuracies. For example, it falls into the most predictable of misunderstandings by stating that artistic artificial intelligence models "store compressed copies of images for training and then recombine them" and thus function as "21st century collage tools".

On April 18, 2023, motions to dismiss[2] were filed by the defendants' attorneys. In summary, in support of the dismissal of the case, it is pointed out that for a copyright infringement claim based on the creation of an alleged derivative work there must be a substantial similarity, whereas in the plaintiffs' briefs it is basically admitted that there is not. Stability AI claims that it is not a "collage" creator at all, but a much more sophisticated learning algorithm that creates new works and not just copies. It reads in fact:

> «Plaintiffs thus falsely equivocate between "derivative work" as a copyright concept, and "derivative work" as a term they made up to describe all output created by Defendants' users. Any infringement claims relying on the former concept must be dismissed for failure to identify a single output by Midjourney that allegedly looks anything like [the] Plaintiffs' Works.»

Stability AI also claims that no evidence was provided that there was any removal of copyright ownership information. Finally, DeviantArt, predictably, defended itself by pointing out that it was not involved in the development of the Stability AI models and the use of the LAION dataset, nor in the removal of copyright ownership information; as DeviantArt was an end user, or licensee, of the Stability AI technology.

The case is very complex and continues to unfold. As of the completion of this book, the most interesting although interim order in this case is the August 12, 2024 order, in which the court granted in part

2 The original document is available at https://www.courtlistener.com/docket/66732129/52/andersen-v-stability-ai-ltd/.

and denied in part the motions to dismiss filed by the defendants.

In summary, the court found sufficient evidence to allow the plaintiffs' claims of direct copyright infringement to proceed. Also, they permitted claims regarding inducement of copyright infringement.

Challenges regarding the intentional removal of Copyright Management Information (so-called CMI) under the DMCA were dismissed with prejudice, meaning that they cannot be resubmitted in subsequent stages of the process.

Interesting is the position publicly expressed by the Copyright Alliance just in commentary on this latest order, the conclusions of which I quote:

> «What Judge Orrick is getting at is similar to something that we at the Copyright Alliance have been stressing when considering the many issues surrounding generative AI. That is, generative AI impacts each copyright industry differently because they operate using different business models, provisions in copyright law apply to them differently, and most important, the AI models that impact them are different. As the order points out, LLMs operate differently than image generators, and they both operate differently than music generator models. It's tempting to generalize and compare the different models and infringement cases, but each involves a very unique set of facts that must be considered independently.»

Given the symbolic importance of this lawsuit and given the interesting issues raised, I suggest the reader keep an eye out for future developments and the various commentary articles by jurists, which will certainly not be lacking.

As Lara Mastrangelo has appropriately noted, everything will come down to the ability of the parties to prove actual copying of the works and not mere similarity in style.

3. Raw Story Media and AlterNet Media vs. OpenAI

On November 7, 2024, Judge McMahon of the United States District Court for the Southern District of New York issued a significant ruling on artificial intelligence and copyright. The ruling addressed one of the most hotly debated and controversial issues in the generative AI landscape: the legality of using copyrighted content to train systems in the absence of specific permission from the rights holders.

The case pitted two companies that own online news outlets and produce news content (namely Raw Story Media Inc. and AlterNet Media Inc.) against the entire OpenAI corporate group (OpenAI Inc., OpenAI GP, LLC, OpenAI, LLC, OpenAI Opco LLC, OpenAI Global LLC and OpenAI Holdings, LLC). The plaintiffs structured their legal action on two separate fronts, seeking two different forms of compensatory protection.

The first claim was based on Section 1202 (b)(I) of the Digital Millennium Copyright Act (DMCA), arguing the unlawful removal of Copyright Management Information (CMI, which we discussed previously) from a copyrighted work constitutes tangible harm.

On the second front, the plaintiffs sought injunctive relief, arguing that there was a substantial risk that OpenAI's system would provide responses to users incorporating material from the plaintiffs' copyrighted works or regurgitating literal or near-literal copyrighted works.

OpenAI's defense focused on a key procedural issue, challenging the plaintiffs' standing under U.S. civil law, thus calling into question the Court's own jurisdiction over the matter. According to OpenAI's lawyers, the legal framework in question would be very clear:

> «Article III standing requires a concrete injury even in the context of a statutory violation. To establish standing, a plaintiff must show: (i) that he suffered an injury in fact that is concrete, particularized, and actual or imminent; (ii) that the injury was likely caused by the defendant; and (ii) that the injury would likely be redressed by judicial relief.»

Importantly, as reflected in the ruling, the party invoking federal jurisdiction bears the burden of establishing these elements. Moreover, standing cannot be treated generically or collectively, but requires a specific showing for each type of relief being sought (e.g., injunction and damages).

Judge McMahon accepted OpenAI's arguments, dismissing the plaintiffs' claims for lack of standing. In his reasoning, he explained that:

> «when a user inputs a question into ChatGPT, ChatGPT synthesizes the relevant information in its repository into an answer. Given the quantity of information contained in the repository, the likelihood that ChatGPT would output plagiarized content from one of Plaintiffs' articles seems remote.»

Although the plaintiffs had submitted statistics for previous versions of ChatGPT that showed a significant presence of plagiarized content, the court found that it had not been plausibly demonstrated that there was a "substantial risk" that the current version of ChatGPT could generate responses that plagiarized the plaintiffs' articles, thus denying standing to seek injunctive relief.

As Massimo Simbula aptly explains in an article commenting on the decision,

> «Pursuant to 17 U.S.C. § 1202(b)(1), it is prohibited to intentionally remove or alter CMI without the permission of the copyright owner, knowing or having reasonable grounds to know that such actions will facilitate, enable, or conceal infringement. A "double-awareness" (double-scienter) standard is required for liability under this provision [...]. In essence, a person must meet two levels of awareness (hence the term double-scienter):
>
> (i) Awareness of Unauthorized Removal or Alteration: the person must know, or have reasonable grounds to know, that copyright management information (e.g., author's name, terms of use, or copyright information) has been removed or altered without the permission of the rights holder.
>
> (ii) Awareness of effect on infringement: The person must know, or have reasonable grounds to know, that removing or altering this information will facilitate, enable, or conceal copyright infringement. In other words, the action must have a direct connection to copyright infringement.»[3]

Thus, it is confirmed that the pain point in these lawsuits is the evidentiary one. With this high threshold imposed by U.S. copyright law, it is always very difficult to succeed in lawsuits for rights holders of works used in training without permission.

---

3 Massimo Simbula, *ChatGPT accusato di rubare articoli, ma il Tribunale dà ragione a OpenAI: il criterio della "doppia consapevolezza"*, 15 November 2024, https://studiolegalesimbula.com/chatgpt-accusato-di-rubare-articoli-ma-il-tribunale-da-ragione-a-openai-il-criterio-della-doppia-consapevolezza/.

The matter may not be over, however. In fact, Raw Story Media and Alter Media could come knocking on the doors of the New York District Court again, filing a new suit that is appropriately supplemented. This would be possible if the publishing companies succeed in gathering sufficient evidence to prove OpenAI's liability under the double-scienter principle outlined above.

4. Robert Kneschke vs. LAION

As we have explained many times, most lawsuits in the field of generative AI systems training take place before American courts. The case brought by Robert Kneschke, on the other hand, is one of the few (at the time of writing of this book) that is entirely European, as it is located in the Hamburg Regional Court in Germany and also hinges on German and European Union law. The case was an interesting first test for the operation of the "text and data mining" exception introduced by Directive 2019/790/EU and its application to the field of artificial intelligence. The decision[4] in the first instance trial came on September 27, 2024.

As we have mentioned, the plaintiff is Robert Kneschke, a professional photographer who complains about the unauthorized use of his images by the defendant LAION eV, an association that has made a dataset with nearly six billion image-text pairs available to the public free of charge. The dataset

4 A well-written summary of the ruling with all the details of the proceedings is available on the WIPO website (see https://www.wipo.int/wipolex/en/text/592042).

consists of a spreadsheet with hyperlinks to publicly available images or image files on the Internet, as well as information about each image, including a textual description (also called alternative text).

According to the evidence in the case, to create that dataset LAION used data from a third party that contained the respective image URLs and text descriptions; it then downloaded the linked images into the existing dataset, used software to check whether the text description matched the corresponding image, and filtered out those in which the text and image did not have a sufficient match. The defendant then extracted the metadata associated with the remaining images, specifically the URL of the image storage location and the image description, to create the new dataset.

As part of this process, an image copyrighted by the plaintiff and made available online through a photo agency's website was recorded, downloaded, analyzed, and included in the new dataset with its metadata. The photo agency, in the terms of use of its website, had set out a limitation under which downloading content from the site using automated programs was prohibited. The plaintiff also asked the defendant to refrain in the future from reproducing the plaintiff's image for the creation of artificial intelligence training datasets.

The court agreed with LAION and disagreed with the photographer's claims, dismissing the court action. It was held that the downloading of the image in the context and manner we have described was to be considered covered by the "text and data mining" exception for the purposes of scientific research conducted by non-commercial research organizations. LAION falls precisely among this type of entity (although it has had dealings with some companies with commercial purposes active in the AI sector), and what is more, it has released the dataset in question freely for all to see.

Text and data mining is defined in German law (which echoes the directive's dictate) as "the automated analysis of single or multiple digital or digitized works in order to extract information from them, particularly about patterns, trends and correlations". The court found that the comparison of the image content with the defendant's description of the pre-existing image fell within this definition.

Moreover, Kneschke failed to show that the exception did not apply.

As Carolina Battistella's timely commentary[5] on the judgment points out (in which the author also speculates on the outcome of a similar case conducted in Italy), the central theme that emerges in this judgment is the mechanism of the so-called "opt-out", that is, the possibility provided by the text and data mining exception to still reserve the right not to authorize the use of one's own works (a kind of exception to the exception, then). As she explains:

> «On this point, the Court stated that exercising the opt-out through plain language [...] is sufficient to allow rights holders to express their reservation. Moreover, it ruled that it is not necessary for the opt-out to be formulated in a machine-readable format, such as robots.txt files, since current technologies, including those based on artificial intelligence, should be able

5 Carolina Battistella, *L'opt-out al training dell'AI con materiale protetto dal diritto d'autore non è illimitato*, 6 December 2024, https://dirittoaldigitale.com/2024/12/06/training-ai/.

to interpret human language. [...] This opening introduces new challenges for companies in the AI sector: if the opt-out formulated with a natural language is considered "machine-readable", AI systems will need to be able to process text written in a human language to identify such reservations.»

Another interesting issue raised by the German judgment is that of the only temporary use of the images. The Hamburg court rejected LAION's defense that the images were used only temporarily and thus under another exception to copyright under German law. According to the court, the reproduction of the images made by LAION could not be considered "transient" or "incidental", because the image files were downloaded and analyzed in a deliberate and intentional manner, showing that the downloading was not just a secondary step in the analysis process, but a conscious and controlled action by LAION.

5. Getty Images Inc vs. Stability AI Inc.

Let us now turn to the case law case involving Getty Images (one of the world's leading photo agencies) as plaintiff and Stability AI as defendant, again. In relation to this case, even before the official court documents were publicly available, statements from Getty Images management were circulating, particularly on TheVerge.com; from these it was possible to immediately deduce that the case concerned a general copyright infringement as well as a violation of the terms of use of Getty Images websites, in particular regarding the prohibition of scraping.

Stable Diffusion's model was trained using a large collection of images (3-5 billion) from LAION, a German-based association set up to provide datasets for use in training artificial intelligence models. This case, therefore, features a familiar entity we encountered earlier when discussing the German case of photographer Robert Kneschke; with the key distinction that this case involves Stability AI, clearly a commercial company, rather than a nonprofit organization.

Interviewed in January 2023[6], Getty Images CEO Craig Peters clarified what their demands were with respect to Stability AI, explaining that they were not so much interested in economic damages or stopping the development of AI art tools, but in creating a new legal status quo presumably with favorable licensing terms for Getty Images.

> «I don't think it's about damages and it's not about stopping the distribution of this technology. I think there are ways of building generative models that respect intellectual property. [...] And that's what we're looking for, rather than a singular entity benefiting of the backs of others. That's the long term goal of this action.»

A few weeks later, in another interview also collected by TheVerge.com[7], more precise details about the contents of the lawsuit emerged. This time we report

6 James Vincent, *Getty Images is suing the creators of AI art tool Stable Diffusion for scraping its content*, 17 January 2023, https://www.theverge.com/2023/1/17/23558516/ai-art-copyright-stable-diffusion-getty-images-lawsuit.

7 James Vincent, *Getty Images sues AI art generator Stable Diffusion in the US for copyright infringement*, 6 February 2023, https://www.theverge.com/2023/2/6/23587393/ai-art-copyright-lawsuit-getty-images-stable-diffusion.

the statement of Anne Flanagan, vice president of communications at Getty Images:

> «We can confirm on Friday Getty Images filed a complaint against Stability AI, Inc. in the United States District Court in Delaware. Getty Images has also filed a Claim in the High Court, which has not been served at this time.»

According to some experts, including, for example, attorney and discloser Aaron Moss, who is among the first to comment on the writ, Getty Images' action is much better argued and focused than the Andersen, McKernan, and Ortiz class action. In a February 4, 2023 tweet he stated:

> «Getty's new complaint is much better than the over-reaching class action lawsuit I wrote about last month. The focus is where it should be: the input stage ingestion of copyrighted images to train the data. This will be a fascinating fair use battle.»[8]

And in an interviewed for TheVerge, Moss added:

> «The action lawsuit was much more focused on the occupational harm caused to working artists by the proliferation of AI tools, while Getty's concentrates on the fact it wasn't paid for the use of its images. Notably, Getty has licensed its images and metadata to other AI art generators, underscoring the fact that Stability AI willfully scraped its images without permission.»

Looking at the images circulated on the net between January and February 2023 actually reveals that some of the images generated by Stable Diffusion almost slavishly reproduce the typical watermark shown on the images disseminated online by Getty Images as a promotional preview. And this indeed seems to

8 Seehttps://x.com/copyrightlately/status/1621678417417736192.

confirm that the system was trained with many of those images in violation of the Getty Images sites' terms of use; if Stability AI had obtained a prior license, it could have used a database with watermark-free images.

Figure 7: on the left, one of the images available on the Getty Images websites with the typical watermark; on the right, an image generated with Stable Diffusion that undoubtedly seems "modeled" on the one on the left and in which a trace of the watermark appears.

So far, we have only outlined the background that then led Getty Images to sue; a lawsuit that, by the way, was filed on two "parallel tracks", one before the United State District Court for the District of Delaware (by complaint dated February 3, 2023[9]), and the other before the United Kingdom's Royal Courts of Justice in London.

Regarding the lawsuit in Delaware, Getty Images initiated the civil case against Stability AI attaching

9 The original document is available at https://zenodo.org/records/7866321.

various documents and evidence and alleging various violations: communication of false copyright management information, removal or alteration of copyright management information, trademark infringement, unfair competition, trademark weakening, and other related contentions under state law. Thus, the scope is not strictly copyright law but other areas of intellectual property law are also touched upon. The case was assigned to Judge Gregory B. Williams.

For its part, Stability AI filed a motion to dismiss, or transfer the case, raising a plea of jurisdiction. The judge ordered Stability AI Ltd. to make some jurisdictional clarifications to evaluate the motion to dismiss.

As of this writing, the proceedings remain stalled on procedural matters, with the core substantive issues yet to be addressed. However, readers are encouraged to keep an eye out for any news with updates[10].

In contrast, the proceedings opened in the United Kingdom, although also not concluded[11], have had some more concrete developments and resulted in an initial decision dated January 14, 2025[12].

In this order, the High Court of Justice, Business and Property Courts of England and Wales, Intellectual Property (Chancery Division) first ruled that Stability AI infringed Getty Images' copyrights

---

10 At https://www.courtlistener.com/docket/66788385/getty-images-us-inc-v-stability-ai-inc/ you can find the step by step progression of the case.

11 An interesting commentary with a well-done reconstruction of the situation that led to the lawsuit can be found in Peter Waters, *Getty Images vs Stability AI*, 25 March 2024, https://www.gtlaw.com.au/insights/getty-images-vs-stability-ai.

12 The original document is available at https://zenodo.org/records/14993002.

by "scraping" millions of images from its websites without consent to train the Stable Diffusion model. It also acknowledged that Stability AI violated Getty Images' database rights by using the collected images to create a training database for its artificial intelligence model. Indeed, remember that, as we have explained, since this is a case referring to the laws of the United Kingdom and not the United States, database protection is more stringent.

The court then addressed Getty Images' trademark and unfair competition profiles, ruling that Stability AI infringed on Getty Images' trademarks because some of the images generated by the Stable Diffusion model contained Getty's watermarks and that Stability AI's actions constituted unfair competition, damaging Getty Images' market and reputation.

Based on these arguments, the court ordered Stability AI to cease using Getty's images for training its model and imposed significant monetary penalties for the damage caused.

As a commentary by Dreyfus Law Firm appropriately notes[13], this decision carries with it important repercussions in two directions; towards those who develop AI systems and towards intellectual property rights holders:

A – For AI development

This case underscores the necessity for AI developers to exercise caution when utilizing third-party materials

13 Dreyfus Law Firm, *Getty Images (US) Inc and Others v. Stability AI Ltd [2025] EWHC 38 (Ch): An interesting case in AI and Intellectual Property Law*, 19 February 2025, https://www.dreyfus.fr/en/2025/02/19/getty-images-us-inc-and-others-v-stability-ai-ltd-2025-ewhc-38-ch-an-interesting-case-in-ai-and-intellectual-property-law/.

in training models. The court's willingness to consider software as an "article" for the purposes of secondary infringement suggests that developers could face liability for unauthorized use of protected works, even in the absence of direct copying.

B – For Intellectual Property rights holders
The decision highlights the challenges IP rights holders face in protecting their works against unauthorized use in AI development. The court's approach to jurisdiction and the interpretation of existing legal frameworks may influence how rights holders structure their agreements and enforcement strategies in the context of emerging technologies.

This UK ruling undoubtedly represents an important victory for Getty Images and sets a significant precedent for future cases concerning the use of copyrighted materials for training artificial intelligence models. Most importantly, it confirms that there is a different sensibility on these issues in European legal systems than in the United States.

Despite this initial result obtained by Getty Images, at the end of May 2025 Craig Peters, CEO of Getty Images, released some statements[14] regarding the legal battle against Stability AI and more generally against companies in the Generative AI sector, which – according to him – are guilty of unfair competition and theft. "We are spending millions of dollars to take on a world of rhetoric", he declared, revealing a certain demotivation towards legal actions that fail to

14 Ryan Browne, *Getty Images spending millions to battle a 'world of rhetoric' in AI suit, CEO says*, 28 May 2025, https://www.cnbc.com/2025/05/28/getty-ceo-stability-ai-lawsuit-doesnt-cover-industry-mass-theft.html.

change things in concrete terms and implying that Getty Images will probably no longer invest many resources in this legal activity.

Peters also explained the difficulties in handling cases like this:

> «I think our case is very strong. But I'm going to caveat that: we had to file in the U.S. and the U.K., and to be candid, we didn't know where this training took place. There are elements where we have to go through and then we've got to spend money for due diligence, and they resist and we've got to fight, and we go back and forth.»

6. New York Times vs. Open AI

A case law case that has gained a lot of visibility in recent months (given the importance of the players involved) is the one between the New York Times and OpenAI, again over issues of artificial intelligence training with copyrighted content and without prior permission.

Indeed, the New York Times claims that OpenAI has been massively scraping millions of its articles and using them to train its artificial intelligence models. The problem in this case is that, the well-known newspaper complains, ChatGPT's models sometimes store parts of the articles included in the training data going so far as to generate almost literal reproductions of the works. The problem then would be much broader, because it would no longer concern only the use of content in training but a real reproduction activity.

Output from GPT-4:
many of America's other global companies — aren't nearly as avid in creating American jobs as other famous companies were in their heydays.
Apple employs 43,000 people in the United States and 20,000 overseas, a small fraction of the over 400,000 American workers at General Motors in the 1950s, or the hundreds of thousands at General Electric in the 1980s. Many more people work for Apple's contractors: an additional 700,000 people engineer, build and assemble iPads, iPhones and Apple's other products. But almost none of them work in the United States. Instead, they work for foreign companies in Asia, Europe and elsewhere, at factories that almost all electronics designers rely upon to build their wares.
"Apple's an example of why it's so hard to create middle-class jobs in the U.S. now," said Jared Bernstein, who until last year was an economic adviser to the White House. "If it's the pinnacle of capitalism, we should be worried."
Apple executives say that going overseas, at this point, is their only option. One former executive described how the company relied upon a Chinese factory to revamp iPhone manufacturing just weeks before the device was due on shelves. Apple had redesigned the iPhone's screen at the last minute, forcing an assembly line overhaul. New screens began arriving at the plant near midnight.
A foreman immediately roused 8,000 workers inside

Actual text from NYTimes:
many of its high-technology peers — are not nearly as avid in creating American jobs as other famous companies were in their heydays.
Apple employs 43,000 people in the United States and 20,000 overseas, a small fraction of the over 400,000 American workers at General Motors in the 1950s, or the hundreds of thousands at General Electric in the 1980s. Many more people work for Apple's contractors: an additional 700,000 people engineer, build and assemble iPads, iPhones and Apple's other products. But almost none of them work in the United States. Instead, they work for foreign companies in Asia, Europe and elsewhere, at factories that almost all electronics designers rely upon to build their wares.
"Apple's an example of why it's so hard to create middle-class jobs in the U.S. now," said Jared Bernstein, who until last year was an economic adviser to the White House.
"If it's the pinnacle of capitalism, we should be worried."
Apple executives say that going overseas, at this point, is their only option. One former executive described how the company relied upon a Chinese factory to revamp iPhone manufacturing just weeks before the device was due on shelves. Apple had redesigned the iPhone's screen at the last minute, forcing an assembly line overhaul. New screens began arriving at the plant near midnight.

Figure 8: On the left, the output provided by ChatGPT; on the right, the text of the original New York Times article.

The case has been filed in the District Court for the Southern District of New York, and as of the date of writing this book, no relevant decision has yet arrived; however, court documents from the parties are available from which the legal issues involved can already be deduced.

As can be easily guessed, OpenAI argues that the use of publicly available materials on the Internet for training artificial intelligence models falls under the concept of "fair use"; and in addition to writing this in the defense briefs in the lawsuit, it writes it in great detail and argument in a well-known statement[15] on the company's official blog.

In its defense, OpenAI refers to an arcane 2015 decision (Authors Guild v. Google, Inc.[16]) that allowed Google to scan millions of copyrighted books to create the Google Books service, applying the principle of fair use. OpenAI basically argues that there is a substantial similarity between the activity carried out at the time by a search engine like Google (which had to acquire and "read" books in order to index them) and the training activity of a generative artificial intelligence system[17]; and that therefore this precedent (and many other similar precedents concerning search engines) would justify the use of copyrighted documents to train generative models.

OpenAI then raises (both in court documents and in public statements and interviews with its managers) a broader issue of advancing science, arguing

15 *OpenAI and journalism*, 8 January 2024, https://openai.com/index/openai-and-journalism/.

16 For more details on the case, see the dedicated Wikipedia entry: https://en.wikipedia.org/wiki/Authors_Guild,_Inc._v._Google,_Inc..

17 However, not everyone agrees on the parallel with the Google Books case. For example, Lee and Grimmelmann in an interesting article shift the focus to another parallel, that with the rulings of the early 2000s on MP3 file exchange platforms: «AI companies are on shakier legal ground than Google was in its book search case. And the courts don't always side with technology companies in cases where companies make copies to build their systems. The story of MP3.com illustrates the kind of legal peril AI companies could face in the coming years.» See Timothy B. Lee and James Grimmelmann, *Why The New York Times might win its copyright lawsuit against OpenAI*, 20 February 2024, https://arstechnica.com/tech-policy/2024/02/why-the-new-york-times-might-win-its-copyright-lawsuit-against-openai/.

that preventing the use of data to train artificial intelligence models would unjustifiably and counter-productively hinder technological development and innovation.

On March 26, 2025, Judge Stein issued an order[18] dismissing some of the New York Times' claims with OpenAI and against Microsoft (also a defendant in the case). However, the rejected claims are not the central ones on direct copyright infringement, and some of them were dismissed "without prejudice", so they may be re-filed at a different stage of the trial. We therefore are kept waiting for the judges to take a position on the main and more "juicy" legal issues.

7. Alan Giana vs. Shein

This case is quite different from the others we have commented on and for that very reason shows profiles of interest.

Usually these lawsuits are directed directly against the companies developing the AI systems, which are accused of training their systems using immense masses of data without obtaining all the proper licenses and thus violating intellectual property rights. The Shein case appears to be different, because precisely who is being sued by Alan Giana is not the one who developed the AI system but rather

18 See Edward Lee, *Judge Stein dismisses some, but not all claims v. OpenAI and Microsoft in the newspapers cases (New York Times, Daily News, Center for Inv. Reporting)*, 26 March 2025, https://chatgptiseatingtheworld.com/2025/03/26/judge-stein-dismisses-some-but-not-all-claims-v-openai-and-microsoft-in-the-newspapers-cases-new-york-times-daily-news-center-for-inv-reporting/.

the one who used it to replicate protected works (Shein precisely).

According to Giana, Shein allegedly used artificial intelligence to recognize and replicate works protected by copyright and registered design rights without permission, and then set in motion a totally parasitic "fast fashion" machine with unfair competition profiles. From what can be understood by reading the complaint[19] written by Giana's lawyers, what Shein does is in fact traceable to an automated system of algorithmic search of creative works and their massive and systematic copying, without any human filter. It reads in fact:

> «To churn out new items at such a fever pitch, the outputs of Shein's algorithm-based design system — in many instances identical copies of copyrighted works — are transmitted directly to Shein's factories for production, with no human intermediary or compliance function taking care that the algorithm's designs are not the property of others.»

This is undoubtedly an interesting scenario, but it brings the issue back to a more classical level of copyright infringement, design rights, trademark rights, and perhaps even unfair competition with unfair business practices; here after all, we are talking more about slavish and massive copying of works and products and not so much about generating works with AI systems.

19 The original document is available at https://zenodo.org/records/13981454.

8. Thomson Reuters vs. ROSS Intelligence

This case, instituted before the U.S. District Court for the District of Delaware, is of particular interest because the court's decision runs counter to other similar cases by not espousing the approach that recognizes general fair use coverage for training activities.

On the one hand we have the company Thomson Reuters (more precisely Thomson Reuters Enterprise Centre GmbH), which makes and markets Westlaw, a major online database for jurists, with laws, regulations, judgments, summaries and excerpts of court decisions and related commentaries. On the other hand, we have ROSS Intelligence, a company that made and trained systems for searching and reorganizing legal materials and closed its doors in 2021 (apparently also due to the backlash from this long and costly lawsuit that began the previous year[20]).

The bone of contention is clearly always the same: the training activity done by ROSS Intelligence by massively exploiting the Thomson Reuters database without specific authorization from the latter. However, unlike the other cases commented on, it does not involve generative artificial intelligence, since precisely ROSS was not making a system similar to ChatGPT or Claude. Among other things, it has been shown that ROSS did not feed its case law research system the texts of Westlaw's case notes in

20 See Robert J. Ambrogi, *Legal Research Company ROSS to Shut Down Under Pressure of Thomson Reuters' Lawsuit*, 11 December 2020, https://www.lawnext.com/2020/12/legal-research-company-ross-to-shut-down-under-pressure-of-thomson-reuters-lawsuit.html.

a massive though temporary copying activity; and it attempted to license the necessary content directly from Thomson Reuters, but the latter refused fearing that ROSS's platform might compete with Westlaw.

In February 2025, the court-appointed judge (Stephanos Bibas) issued a ruling (precisely, a Memorandum Opinion[21]) in which he retraced his steps from an earlier ruling in 2023 and in which he rejected ROSS' defenses entirely by ruling out fair use coverage.

The fact that this decision runs counter to others on the application of fair use should not surprise us all that much. Rather, it is a confirmation of what we have already explained at length, namely that U.S. fair use is a legal institution that always requires a precise case-by-case assessment. And as already explained, this case has substantial differences from the others.

The decision among other things is objectionable in several respects, which are brought into sharp and lucid focus by Martin Adams for Authorsalliance.org[22]. In the article Adams concludes:

> «The impact of this case is currently limited, both because it is a district court ruling and because it concerns non-generative AI. However, it is important to remain vigilant, as the reasoning put forth by the ROSS court could influence other judges, policymakers, and even the broader public, if left unchallenged. This ruling combines several problematic arguments

21 The original document is available at https://zenodo.org/records/14936656.

22 Martin Adams, *Thomson Reuters v. ROSS: the first AI fair use ruling fails to persuade*, 13 February 2025, https://www.authorsalliance.org/2025/02/13/thomson-reuters-v-ross-the-first-ai-fair-use-ruling-fails-to-persuade/.

that, if accepted more widely, could have significant consequences.»

The issues raised in the article are closely related to the various nuances of American fair use and are very complex. I therefore refer back to reading the original source for a more thorough understanding.

9. Disney, Universal et al. vs. Midjourney

At the time of writing this book, we do not yet have complete information on this lawsuit, which was announced in mid-June 2025; however, given the importance of the issues at stake and the subjects involved, we cannot avoid making a few mentions.

The two Hollywood majors are complaining in particular about copyright infringement on their famous fictional characters (including the ogre Shrek, the superhero Spider-Man, but also Darth Vader and the Minions) that Midjourney's AI is able to reproduce flawlessly after a simple text prompt. According to the plaintiffs' lawyers, this would be incontrovertible proof that Midjourney's algorithm was trained with thousands of images taken from films, comics and drawings without any authorization, leveraging the principle of fair use.

The complaint[23] filed with the Central District of California (Los Angeles) is accompanied by a file that contains many side-by-side comparisons between the original copyrighted characters and the images generated by Midjourney.

23 The original document is available at https://zenodo.org/records/15847137.

As Boyar Miller explains very clearly in his commentary on the complaint, the key legal issues of this case are essentially three: i) direct and secondary infringement; ii) willful and systematic infringement; iii) profit motive and commercial harm.

The intent of this case is therefore to demonstrate that in reality the authorization by the copyright holders is always necessary and that fair use is not sufficient, as happened in the case Thomson Reuters vs ROSS Intelligence.

On the potential impact of this case, the point of view expressed by Andrew R. Chow on The Time[24] is interesting and deserves careful reading:

> «If the Disney-Universal lawsuit is similarly successful, that would have major implications for both AI and Hollywood, says Naeem Talukdar, the CEO of the AI video startup Moonvalley. Many AI companies might have to retrain their visual models from the ground up with licensed content. And Hollywood, if given legal clarity, might actually accelerate its usage of AI models built upon licensed content, like ones built by Moonvalley and Natasha Lyonne's and Bryn Mooser's Asteria Film Co.»

10. Bartz et al. vs. Anthropic

Certainly, due to the high-profile names involved, the case discussed in the previous paragraph attracts considerable attention from readers; but in terms

---

24 Andrew R. Chow, *How the Disney-Midjourney Lawsuit Could Reshape the Battle Over AI and Copyright*, 11 June 2025, https://time.com/7293362/disney-universal-midjourney-lawsuit-ai/.

of legal impact, the decision[25] published on June 23, 2025, by the United States District Court for the Northern District of California will likely become one of the most interesting and illuminating precedents.

The plaintiffs are authors of literary works (Andrea Bartz, Charles Graeber, and Kirk Wallace Johnson) who sued Anthropic (the company that created Claude.ai) for training their systems with millions of literary works without the consent of the authors and publishers. As in all other similar legal cases, the court was called upon to determine whether the defendant's uses are covered by the fair use principle or constitute an outright copyright violation.

Anthropic trained its artificial intelligence both with seven million works from repositories that we can consider "pirate" (such as Books3, LibGen, and PiLiMi), and by digitizing millions of hard copies of books that were regularly acquired. In the digitization process, the hard copies were destroyed: bindings were stripped so that pages could be scanned more easily, and then, once digitized, those pages were sent to be pulped. This dual method of acquiring and using copyrighted work allowed the judge to treat the two distinct cases with different approaches, analyzing them separately and providing an innovative interpretation of fair use doctrine.

As Thomas James explains[26],

> «The print copies were then discarded. The digital copies were not distributed to others. Under these circumstances, the court ruled that making digital

25 The original document is available at https://zenodo.org/records/15847017.

26 Thomas James, *AI OK; Piracy Not: Bartz v. Anthropic*, 25 June 2025, https://thomasbjames.com/ai-ok-piracy-not-bartz-v-anthropic/.

> versions of print books is fair use. [...] The authors did not contend that Claude generated infringing output. Instead, they argued that copies of their works were used as inputs to train the AI. The Copyright Act, however, does not prohibit or restrict the reading or analysis of copyrighted works. So long as a copy is lawfully purchased, the owner of the purchased copy can read it and think about it as often as he or she wishes.»

Indeed, for our reflection, the most interesting passage of the ruling is where the judge confirms the parallel between the study and analysis of a text done by a human being and the study and analysis of a text done instead by an AI system.

The most interesting passage of the judge's decision is the following:

> «Authors further argue that the training was intended to memorize their works' creative elements — not just their works' non-protectable ones. But this is the same argument. Again, Anthropic's LLMs have not reproduced to the public a given work's creative elements, nor even one author's identifiable expressive style (assuming arguendo that these are even copyrightable). Yes, Claude has outputted grammar, composition, and style that the underlying LLM distilled from thousands of works. But if someone were to read all the modern-day classics because of their exceptional expression, memorize them, and then emulate a blend of their best writing, would that violate the Copyright Act? Of course not. Copyright does not extend to "methods of operation, concepts, or principles illustrated or embodied in a work.»

The judge's reasoning truly seems in line with many of the points I have proposed in this book and confirms a key concept: the training of AI systems has concrete similarities to human learning; therefore, it is quite complicated to treat differently the use of creative works by humans to learn how to create other works and the text and data mining done on creative works to train generative AI.

But the most interesting twist in this legal proceeding occurred in mid-July 2025 (when the drafts of this book were actually about to be closed). In an order dated July 17, Judge William Alsup ruled that the authors can file a class action lawsuit on behalf of all US writers whose copyrights have been infringed because Anthropic extracted their works from pirated libraries.

This is a very dangerous legal turn for Anthropic, which some say could lead to it having to pay out monstrous compensation to thousands of stakeholders; this compensation could lead to the company's bankruptcy[27]. An Anthropic spokesperson said that the company is considering appealing this decision, as the court failed to take many factors into account. I therefore urge readers to monitor the news on this legal matter for further developments.

27 A complete and detailed commentary on this decision is available (once again) on the Chat GPT Is Eating the World blog by Edward Lee, at https://chatgptiseatingtheworld.com/2025/07/17/anthropic-faces-potential-business-ending-liability-in-statutory-damages-after-judge-alsup-certifies-class-action-by-bartz/ . The post provides a detailed table calculating the hypothetical damages Anthropic would be required to pay if the class action were to succeed.

11. Kadrey et al. vs. Meta Platforms

Finally, we arrive at the most recent decision, published on June 25, 2025[28], just a few days before the editorial deadline of this book. It was also issued by the United States District Court for the Northern District of California and more precisely is an "order denying the plaintiffs' motion for partial summary judgment and granting meta's cross-motion for partial summary judgment".

The Plaintiffs are a group of thirteen book authors (including novelist Richard Kadrey and comedian Sarah Silverman) who sued Meta Platforms for training AI models (LLAMA) with many literary works without obtaining legitimate licenses.

The facts and theoretical foundations of the case seem quite consistent with those of the case presented in the previous paragraph, although the scope and effects of the decision are partly different. Plaintiffs contend that Llama is capable of reproducing small snippets of text from their books; they also contend that Meta, by using their works for training without permission, has diminished the authors' ability to license their works for the purpose of training large language models.

According to the Court, "both of these arguments are clear losers" and explains:

> «Llama is not capable of generating enough text from the plaintiffs' books to matter, and the plaintiffs are not entitled to the market for licensing their works as AI training data. As for the potentially winning argument—that Meta has copied their works to create a

---

28 The original document is available at https://zenodo.org/records/15847228.

> product that will likely flood the market with similar works, causing market dilution—the plaintiffs barely give this issue lip service, and they present no evidence about how the current or expected outputs from Meta's models would dilute the market for their own works.»

Here too, the usual problem emerges: to obtain an injunctive relief, solid proof of copyright violation is necessary; proof that is extremely difficult to provide according to US trial criteria. Consequently, Meta emerges victorious, obtaining confirmation that its use of literary works to train its AI does not in itself lead to copyright violation.

The judge's argument proceeds by explaining that, given how the civil lawsuit was structured, the decision cannot have very different outcomes. At the same time, however, the judge warns about the legal scope of this decision and emphasizes that it cannot have very broad effects since it is not a class action.

> «Given the state of the record, the Court has no choice but to grant summary judgment to Meta on the plaintiffs' claim that the company violated copyright law by training its models with their books. But in the grand scheme of things, the consequences of this ruling are limited. This is not a class action, so the ruling only affects the rights of these thirteen authors—not the countless others whose works Meta used to train its models. And, as should now be clear, this ruling does not stand for the proposition that Meta's use of copyrighted materials to train its language models is lawful. It stands only for the proposition that these plaintiffs made the wrong arguments and failed to develop a record in support of the right one.»

The entire text of the decision is interesting (and for this reason I invite you to read it in its entirety). In particular, in the paragraph "II. Facts and procedural history", the judge demonstrates a high understanding of how generative AI works; and this gives positive hope for future trends in American jurisprudence called upon to regulate this very delicate matter.

Finally, entering into the merits of the central theme of fair use, the Court, citing the precedent of Authors Guild v. Google several times (which we have discussed extensively), clarifies in what terms we can find a sufficient level of transformativeness in the training done by META.

On page 21 of the Order we read:

> «The last issue relating to the character of Meta's use (and thus the first factor) is the relationship between Meta's downloading of the plaintiffs' books and Meta's use of the books to train Llama. To the extent the plaintiffs suggest that the former must be considered wholly separately from the latter, they are wrong. To be sure, Meta's downloading is a different use from any copying done in the course of LLM training. But that downloading must still be considered in light of its ultimate, highly transformative purpose: training Llama. See Authors Guild v. Google, Inc. (Google Books) [...] Because Meta's ultimate use of the plaintiffs' books was transformative, so too was Meta's downloading of those books.»

Chapter 5 – The protection of works created with generative AI systems

1. Introduction

To begin with, an important premise that should be clear by now, following our explanation in the first chapter: the founding requirement of copyright is the creative character, therefore creations that are so essential and so banal that they do not denote the minimum of originality required by the legal system remain outside of protection. And this principle applies both to works created with artificial intelligence and to works created through – so to speak – traditional methods. The drawing of a green equilateral triangle would not be considered protectable, whether created by a human or generated by an AI system (via the prompt "draw a green equilateral triangle"). The same applies to mundane texts that merely reproduce standard and unavoidable clichés; or to musical pieces consisting only of a base that is not sufficiently structured and therefore lacking melody, rhythm and harmony.

Consequently, before asking ourselves how to protect the outputs of AI systems, we should start by discriminating between what can be protected and what would still be excluded, therefore in the public domain and freely usable by anyone without constraints.

Then there is the dilemma that we have already investigated several times, that is, whether there can already exist works created entirely by artificial intelligence without any guidance and supervision by humans. A central and decisive dilemma given that, as already clarified for animals, non-human entities and in this case also artificial ones cannot be the owners of copyright.

Finally, we need to understand who the actual owner of the rights is, especially in those cases in which the human intellectual contribution remains very marginal.

2. Can a machine be the owner of intellectual property rights?

Let's begin by restating what we have already emphasized throughout: machines certainly cannot own intellectual property rights. This can also be deduced with mere common sense but, if that were not enough, it has also been clarified in case law. The (negative) provisions obtained in the USA by Thaler have had a fair amount of reverberation and, despite their "temerity", have in fact had the merit of leading to official provisions that have then represented a fixed point for case law. Even the US administrative authority responsible for overseeing the field of patents for invention (United States Patent and Trademark Office, or USPTO) has had the opportunity to express itself in official documents maintaining the same line: a software, an algorithm, a robot, cannot be considered an inventor and therefore cannot be the owner of the patent exclusivity:

> «The USPTO interpretation of the Patent Act was carefully considered and was consistent with the language of the Patent Act and with case law. [...] Accordingly, the USPTO›s interpretation that an 'inventor' must be a natural person is entitled to deference.»

This was stated by the Virginia Eastern District Court in its ruling[1] issued on September 2, 2021 on Thaler's appeal against the USPTO, which had rejected a patent application listing DABUS (acronym for Device for the Autonomous Bootstrapping of Unified Sentience) as the inventor, i.e. the name of the artificial intelligence software created by Thaler himself[2]. This orientation was also confirmed by the case law of the United Kingdom in December 2023 with the decision [2023] UKSC 49[3].

Similar conclusions have also been reached on the copyright level. All attempts to have artificial intelligence recognized as having an authorial role have failed due to the clear position expressed by the USCO. Here too we see Stephan Thaler as the protagonist, who has continued his quixotic battle in the realm of creative works and copyright.

He filed an application for copyright registration with the United States Copyright Office (USCO)

---

1 The original document is available at https://zenodo.org/records/14995418.

2 For more information, see the Wikipedia entry https://en.wikipedia.org/wiki/DABUS.

3 See *Thaler (Appellant) v Comptroller-General of Patents, Designs and Trade Marks (Respondent); Case: [2023] UKSC 49, on appeal from [2021] EWCA Civ 1374*; full text available at https://supremecourt.uk/uploads/uksc_2021_0201_judgment_3f445a5dc7.pdf.

for a work of visual art entitled A Recent Entrance to Paradise. The work in question had been entirely produced by an artificial intelligence system called "Creativity Machine", of which Thaler himself was the developer and owner. In the registration application, Thaler indicated this "machine" as the author of the work, requesting however that the rights of use be attributed to himself.

The USCO remained consistent with the positions expressed on other occasions, rejecting Thaler's application and basing its decision on the impossibility of granting copyright protection to works that did not present any human creative contribution in their creation.

Not satisfied with this response, Thaler first filed an internal administrative appeal asking the USCO to review the decision. However, he was disappointed again and so in June 2022 he decided to appeal the decision to the District Court for the District of Columbia (Washington, DC), arguing that the Copyright Office's decision was characterized by arbitrariness and conflicted with the provisions of the Copyright Act of 1976.

In particular, Thaler wanted to highlight that the law does not contain any provision that explicitly imposes the human nature of the author as a requirement for copyright protection. He also emphasized that the Copyright Act presented an opening towards technological innovations, since it extends its protection to "original works of authorship fixed in tangible expressive media now known or to be developed in the future".

The District Court, in a decision[4] published on August 18, 2023, ruled that, since the US copyright law protects only works of human creation, the USCO did not err in rejecting Thaler's copyright registration application.

The judge noted that, although copyright law has proven sufficiently malleable to adapt to works involving new technologies, human creativity remains the essential condition at the heart of copyright protection, even if such human creativity is channeled through new tools or in new media. According to the Court, copyright has never extended to protect works generated by new forms of technology that operate in the absence of a guiding human hand, as Thaler urges.

Under § 102(a) of the US Copyright Act, copyright protection extends to "original works of authorship fixed in any tangible medium of expression, now known or hereafter developed, from which they can be perceived, reproduced, or otherwise communicated, directly or by the aid of a machine or device".

Although the critical word "author" is not defined in the US Copyright Act, the Court does not seem to want to question the requirement of human input at all and reiterates it in several passages of the ruling. In particular in this one:

> «The critical word "author" is not defined in the Copyright Act. "Author", in its relevant sense, means "one that is the source of some form of intellectual or creative work", "[t]he creator of an artistic work; a

4 The original document is available at the URL https://zenodo.org/records/8268001; while an unofficial summary is available on the WIPO website at https://www.wipo.int/wipolex/en/text/588769.

> painter, photographer, filmmaker, etc." [...] By its plain text, the 1976 Act thus requires a copyrightable work to have an originator with the capacity for intellectual, creative, or artistic labor. Must that originator be a human being to claim copyright protection? The answer is yes. The 1976 Act's "authorship" requirement as presumptively being human rests on centuries of settled understanding.»

And a few paragraphs further on, referring instead to the previous American copyright law (that of 1909):

> «The understanding that "authorship" is synonymous with human creation has persisted even as the copyright law has otherwise evolved. The immediate precursor to the modern copyright law – the Copyright Act of 1909 – explicitly provided that only a "person" could "secure copyright for his work" under the Act. [...] Copyright under the 1909 Act was thus unambiguously limited to the works of human creators.»

Thaler's attempts to "adjust the course" in the case by claiming that he "instructed and directed his AI to create the work", that "the AI is entirely under [his] control", and that "the AI operates only under [his] direction", thereby implying that he played a controlling role in generating the work, directly contradict the findings of the USCO administrative proceeding.

The Court therefore concludes that USCO acted properly in denying a copyright registration for a work created without any human involvement.

Despite all this, Thaler remained dissatisfied and appealed the District Court's ruling in 2024. However, the United States Court of Appeals for the

District of Columbia Circuit, in its decision[5] of March 18, 2025, once again upheld the correctness of the first instance decision and the USCO's actions.

On the same subject and with a similar legal orientation, we cannot fail to mention the "trailblazing" case of Zarya of the Dawn[6], a graphic novel created by author Kris Kashtanova with extensive AI support for the graphics (specifically Midjourney). Upon Kashtanova's request to register the work, the USCO granted a sort of "partial copyright", with protection limited to the concept of the work and the textual part, but not to the individual images generated with AI.

Finally, an interesting and more recent case law comes from another important part of the world: China. The case, concerning the protection of an image generated with Stable Diffusion, had as plaintiff Mr. Li who had generated the image and as defendant a blogger who had reused the image without the prior consent of the plaintiff. The Beijing Internet Court recognized the ownership of the rights to the plaintiff and did so by attributing particular centrality to the so-called prompt.

5 The original document is available at https://zenodo.org/records/15847247.

6 The USCO decision is available at https://www.copyright.gov/docs/zarya-of-the-dawn.pdf. There are several comments on the case by authoritative jurists online, including Atreya Mathur, *Copyright Registration for AI Generated Works: Zarya of the Dawn and the Dawn of a New Creator*, 6 July 2023, https://itsartlaw.org/2023/07/06/copyright-registration-for-ai-generated-works-zarya-of-the-dawn-and-the-dawn-of-a-new-creator/.

3. The U.S. Copyright Office guidelines

Following the initial spread of ChatGPT and other major generative AI platforms, and amid the heated and often contradictory debate about copyright implications, the US Copyright Office (USCO) thought it appropriate to explicitly clarify its position; on March 10, 2023, it published a document that, while reiterating concepts that we have now focused on, provides a first solid and authoritative reference, among other things citing some illuminating examples taken from the practice of its offices.

The document is entitled "Copyright Registration Guidance: Works Containing Material Generated by Artificial Intelligence"[7] and we report a fairly substantial excerpt in Italian translation, accompanied by some comments.

Let's start with paragraph I (Background) which reports some really interesting examples of registration requests received by the USCO from people who have used generative artificial intelligence systems in various capacities to create works:

> «the Office is already receiving and examining applications for registration that claim copyright in AI-generated material. For example, in 2018 the Office received an application for a visual work that the applicant described as "autonomously created by a computer algorithm running on a machine".
> The application was denied because, based on the applicant's representations in the application, the

7 USCO, *Copyright Registration Guidance: Works Containing Material Generated by Artificial Intelligence*, 10 March 2023, https://www.federalregister.gov/documents/2023/03/16/2023-05321/copyright-registration-guidance-works-containing-material-generated-by-artificial-intelligence.

examiner found that the work contained no human authorship. After a series of administrative appeals, the Office's Review Board issued a final determination affirming that the work could not be registered because it was made "without any creative contribution from a human actor".
More recently, the Office reviewed a registration for a work containing human-authored elements combined with AI-generated images. In February 2023, the Office concluded that a graphic novel comprised of human-authored text combined with images generated by the AI service Midjourney constituted a copyrightable work, but that the individual images themselves could not be protected by copyright.
The Office has received other applications that have named AI technology as the author or co-author of the work or have included statements in the "Author Created" or "Note to Copyright Office" sections of the application indicating that the work was produced by or with the assistance of AI. Other applicants have not disclosed the inclusion of AI-generated material but have mentioned the names of AI technologies in the title of the work or the "acknowledgments" section of the deposit.
Based on these developments, the Office concludes that public guidance is needed on the registration of works containing AI-generated content.»

We then move on to section III (The Office's Application of the Human Authorship Requirement) in which the Office addresses the delicate issue of attributing human authorship to these works:

«As the agency overseeing the copyright registration system, the Office has extensive experience in evaluating works submitted for registration that contain human authorship combined with uncopyrightable material, including material generated by or with the assistance of technology. It begins by asking "whether

> the 'work' is basically one of human authorship, with the computer [or other device] merely being an assisting instrument, or whether the traditional elements of authorship in the work (literary, artistic, or musical expression or elements of selection, arrangement, etc.) were actually conceived and executed not by man but by a machine.
>
> In the case of works containing AI-generated material, the Office will consider whether the AI contributions are the result of "mechanical reproduction" or instead of an author's "own original mental conception, to which [the author] gave visible form".
>
> The answer will depend on the circumstances, particularly how the AI tool operates and how it was used to create the final work. This is necessarily a case-by-case inquiry. If a work's traditional elements of authorship were produced by a machine, the work lacks human authorship and the Office will not register it.
>
> [...] In other cases, however, a work containing AI-generated material will also contain sufficient human authorship to support a copyright claim. For example, a human may select or arrange AI-generated material in a sufficiently creative way that "the resulting work as a whole constitutes an original work of authorship". Or an artist may modify material originally generated by AI technology to such a degree that the modifications meet the standard for copyright protection.
>
> In these cases, copyright will only protect the human-authored aspects of the work, which are "independent of" and do "not affect" the copyright status of the AI-generated material itself.»

The situation remains unclear, however, as the USCO points out the need to verify from time to time whether and to what extent there is a human contribution.

Finally, the document concludes with some practical guidance for those who wish to submit an application to the Office for registration of creative works:

> «Individuals who use AI technology in creating a work may claim copyright protection for their own contributions to that work. They must use the Standard Application, and in it identify the author(s) and provide a brief statement in the "Author Created" field that describes the authorship that was contributed by a human. For example, an applicant who incorporates AI-generated text into a larger textual work should claim the portions of the textual work that is human-authored. And an applicant who creatively arranges the human and non-human content within a work should fill out the "Author Created" field to claim: "Selection, coordination, and arrangement of [describe human-authored content] created by the author and [describe AI content] generated by artificial intelligence". Applicants should not list an AI technology or the company that provided it as an author or co-author simply because they used it when creating their work.»

In early 2025, USCO released another important document titled "Copyright and Artificial Intelligence. Part 2: Copyrightability"[8], which provides clarification on the proper classification of works created with generative AI and on the ownership of rights. The document is based on the results of a Notice of Inquiry that collected several questions from users (called "commenters") and which stimulated the reflections of USCO copyright experts:

8 USCO, *Copyright and Artificial Intelligence. Part 2: Copyrightability*, January 2025, https://www.copyright.gov/ai/.

> «Many commenters expressed concern about continuing the longstanding and growing use of computer-assisted tools in the creation process. They pointed to various tasks that have been performed in creative fields for years, some of which now incorporate recent developments in AI, such as "aging" or "de-aging" actors, identifying chord progressions, detecting errors in software code, and removing unwanted objects or crowds from a scene. Commenters argued that these types of uses of AI should not affect the availability of copyright protection for the output.»

In essence, the risk of a drift is being flagged that worries creative professionals. Given that a good part of creative activities will now pass in one way or another to artificial intelligence technologies, the principle that all these activities would no longer be protected because they are mostly performed by software should not pass; on the contrary, it should be emphasized that the intervention of the software is still guided and governed by the human being. The USCO brief on this concern argues:

> «The Office agrees that there is an important distinction between using AI as a tool to assist in the creation of works and using AI as a stand-in for human creativity. While assistive uses that enhance human expression do not limit copyright protection, uses where an AI system makes expressive choices require further analysis. This distinction depends on how the system is being used, not on its inherent characteristics.»

4. It is always a question of autonomy

We have therefore understood that in order for copyright to be recognized, it must be works created

WITH artificial intelligence and not works created BY artificial intelligence. This choice of the correct preposition is obviously a simplification, but it effectively communicates the crux of the matter. We are almost always dealing with works created by humans using artificial intelligence systems, where the human is responsible for preparing, initiating, directing, guiding, and controlling the generative process and therefore assumes the role of author, even if in a new conception of author (as we have already argued extensively in the first chapter).

However, we cannot dismiss the issue so quickly, since it is often not possible to clearly distinguish the human contribution from the machine's contribution in complex creative works; and above all, various creative experiments of works created by (and here I specifically use the preposition "by") unsupervised generative artificial intelligence systems have already emerged, which raise non-trivial philosophical and legal questions.

4.1. What rights over works supervised by a human user?

From the documents discussed in the previous paragraphs, it's clear that the law tends to include generative artificial intelligence systems in the large family of technological tools specifically designed to facilitate creative activity, like graphics, photo editing, and music editing software. A graphic designer using Photoshop to create an advertising poster is the author of the work, with the software serving merely as a tool under their control. With generative AI systems, the situation differs, as a significant portion of expressing the creative idea is performed by software with considerable autonomy; however, it is assumed that the creative act always and in any case occurs under the supervision of a human user, as we have already explained in various passages.

This specific principle doesn't appear to need particular jurisprudential confirmation; rather, parameters will need to be established when there is human supervision or when in reality there is none and the work has been "thrown out" by the AI and published without any human intervention.

However, we can reference a recent Italian legal precedent: an order issued by the First Civil Section of the Supreme Court of Cassation on January 16, 2023 (Ord. n. 1107/2023)[9].

The case involved RAI (the Italian national radio and television company) and Chiara Biancheri (a freelance architect), who appeared before the Supreme Court after a trial brought before the Court of Genoa in 2016, which was then appealed. The dispute centered on the image of a stylised flower with geometric themes, created by Biancheri, distributed online by her and then used by RAI as the graphic theme of the scenography of the music show Sanremo 2016, without the author's permission having been asked.

RAI complained that:

> «the Court of Appeal erroneously classified as a work of the mind an image generated by software and not attributable to a creative idea of its supposed author. The appellant claims that the work of the architect Biancheri is a digital image, with a floral subject, a

9 The complete text of the decision is available at https://aliprandi.blogspot.com/2023/04/ordinanza-rai-utilizzo-immagine-AI-scenografia-sanremo2016.html.

> so-called "fractal" figure, i.e. characterized by self-similarity, or by repetition of its forms on different scales of size and was elaborated by a software, which elaborated its shape, colors and details through mathematical algorithms; the alleged author would have only chosen an algorithm to apply and approved a posteriori the result generated by the computer.»

The Court, however, responds to this complaint by RAI by emphasizing that, in order to contest the absence of creative character in a graphic work such as the one at issue in the judgment,

> «it is not sufficient for the opposing party to have used software to generate the image, a circumstance which, as the appellant itself admits, is still compatible with the development of a work of the mind with a level of creativity that should only be scrutinized with greater rigor.»

Essentially, this confirms the well-known principle that when creative work results from an automated, computerized process, the creative character may undoubtedly be there; at most, it must be verified by proceeding on a case-by-case basis and keeping the bar high in the evaluation.

The order was improperly announced as a first decision on copyright in the field of generative artificial intelligence. In fact, for procedural reasons, the Court of Cassation did not have the opportunity to delve into the specific merits of the issues of "so-called digital art (also called digital art or computer art) as an artistic practice that uses digital technology as part of the creative process or exhibition presentation". Therefore, we cannot consider it a landmark precedent that establishes new legal principles. However, the order was an excellent opportunity to reiterate some key concepts relating to creativity mediated by software or a machine.

What rights are granted to the human user who creates work using an AI system? They receive all the rights typically accorded to authors of intellectual works under the legal system. Under the European legal framework, these include: the right to publish the work, reproduce it, transcribe it, perform, represent or recite it in public, the right to communicate the work to the public, the right to distribute the work, the right to translate, elaborate and modify the work (making derivative works), the right to rent and lend the work.

All these rights are automatically granted to the author upon creation of the work, the moment the creative idea takes form as an intellectual work. It is therefore not necessary to deposit or register it with a public office; the registration only has a probative function of the existence of the work on a specific date (useful in the event of a dispute over paternity between two or more contenders) but does not have a constitutive function of the right.

Additionally, as we'll examine later, the terms of service for major generative AI platforms assign users both responsibility for and ownership rights to the outputs generated. Therefore, if there were doubts about the legal qualification of the user of these platforms as an author, we can move to the contractual level to have greater clarity; the terms of use are in fact the contract that regulates the relationship between the service provider (the company that created and manages the AI system) and the user (the human being who gives the instructions to generate the work).

In Europe, we must also take into account the so-called moral rights of the author, that is, those rights that protect the work more from a personal rather than a patrimonial point of view, rights that create a link between the author and his works on a moral and reputational level. According to the Italian model, they are the right to claim paternity of the work, the right to have one's status as an author recognized in court even in the case of anonymous or pseudonymous works, the right to the integrity of the work (more precisely, the right to oppose modifications to the work that are prejudicial to the honor or reputation of the author), and the right to withdraw the work from the market for serious moral reasons.

Based on the reflections proposed in the first chapter on a new idea of creativity in the era of artificial intelligence, perhaps it is time to ask: does it really make sense to talk about moral rights in works in which a good part of the work is done by the machine and in which the intellectual contribution of the author is more in the form of supervision? Can works of this kind really reflect the author's personality, his creative approach, his way of seeing, his style?

I intentionally leave these questions open, as judicial guidance would be necessary to chart a path forward. Certainly, we already have jurisprudential orientations according to which, in creations where the level of creativity is reduced because the author must stay within predetermined and necessary boundaries (such as software development or the creation of databases), the role of moral rights remains marginal.

4.2. What rights over unsupervised works?

If copyright protection always depends on the control and supervision that the human user has over artificial intelligence, how should we frame the works created by an AI system without a palpable human contribution (although this is still not a very common hypothesis)? Should they truly be considered public domain works, or should we presume some form of legal protection exists? And who would be the owner of this right? The company that produced the AI system? And in what terms?

Consider a familiar example: weather forecasts. The maps with icons that communicate the forecast and the related numerical data (temperatures, atmospheric pressure, etc.) are often generated by a computer that is in direct communication with a meteorological satellite and the level of human intervention in the processing and in the graphic representation of the output is really minimal, if not non-existent. Yet these system outputs represent works requiring substantial investment in time, labor, and technical expertise (typically considered protectable at minimum as datasets subject to sui generis rights).

However, this example concerns a work of a technical-scientific nature and does not create particular disorientation for us. Anyway, cutting-edge generative AI systems can also produce artistic and expressive works designed for entertainment or aesthetic purposes. Should these be treated equivalently to weather forecast maps? Can we treat them in the same way as the weather forecast map?

Laura Chimienti offers a useful perspective here[10], envisioning a scenario in which the subject who created the generative artificial intelligence system (which the author in her essay calls a "digital breeder") holds a right on the outputs since it is the subject who created the conditions for the system to generate the work and has control of the creative process. This right, although in fact it would still behave like a reproduction right, would not however be classifiable as a copyright in the strict sense since there is no author or real authorial activity.

This right would more closely resemble a related right; indeed, Chimienti draws a parallel with film producers who, although not a subject who performs creative acts in the strict sense, is nevertheless the subject who holds the reins of the making of a film and, at least in Italian law, becomes ex lege the pivotal subject of the management of all the rights of use on the film. Alternatively, such a right could be classified as a sui generis right on a par with that reserved for the creators of databases established by Directive 96/9/EC and, in a certain sense, the new right of publishers of journalistic publications established by Directive 2019/790/EU.

While interesting, these classifications remain theoretical proposals from a single scholar; moreover, since it is the creation of a new exclusive right never contemplated by the legal system, a specific legislative intervention in this sense would be necessary and a mere confirmation in case law would not be sufficient.

10 Laura Chimienti, *Diritto di Autore 4.0. L'intelligenza artificiale crea?*, Pacini Editore, 2020; in particular see Chapter IV, paragraphs 1.5 and 1.6.

On this topic, it may be significant to mention the approach of British law which – as we have already mentioned – in the Copyright, Designs and Patents Act (CDPA) of 1988 provides for the concept of computer-generated works (CGW), literally "works generated by the computer". According to the definition of Section 178, computer-generated work means that "the work is generated by the computer in circumstances such that there is no human author of the work". It is therefore a concept that does not coincide with that of computer-assisted works, that is, works created by a human being with the assistance of a computer.

As Jyh-An Lee[11] rightly points out in dealing with the topic in a very noteworthy monograph, with the increasing application of artificial intelligence (AI), copyright disputes associated with computer-generated works have become even more complicated.

The UK's approach on this topic in fact differs from the main international practices on copyright, in which human creative input remains essential for the protection of copyright. The underlying idea is to reserve protection linked to the investment made and the effort (the famous "labour") used to create, train and maintain the artificial intelligence system. It is controversial whether this particular right, which – let us remember – is only provided for in British law, should be classified as a copyright or more properly as a related right. Furthermore, it is always quite

---

11 Jyh-An Lee, *Computer-generated Works under the CDPA 1988*, Chapter 8 in Jyh-An Lee, Reto Hilty, Kung-Chung Liu (editors), *Artificial Intelligence and Intellectual Property*, Oxford University Press, 2021, https://academic.oup.com/book/39560/chapter/339432200.

complicated to establish who the true owner of this right is: the owner of the machine, or the person who activated it, or the person who invested in its creation and training?

As it is easy to note, the emerging doubts regarding the UK model (also reported by British jurists on several occasions[12]) are the same ones that we have already raised in our reflection. In any case, there is no doubt that this right has become increasingly central in recent years. Is it perhaps a legal model that other legal systems can also draw inspiration from? Posterity will decide.

---

12 In particular, see the excellent critique in Nicholas Gervassis and Alina Trapova, *UKIPO's public consultation on AI and IP – computer-generated works (Part 1)*, 14 March 2022, https://copyrightblog.kluweriplaw.com/2022/03/14/ukipos-public-consultation-on-ai-and-ip-computer-generated-works-part-1/.

FOCUS

Copyright and training of AI systems

The main legal cases currently underway focus on the *potential* copyright infringement resulting from training activities carried out with works and data taken from the Internet (and without the prior consent of the rights holders).

Please note that:

- Most of these cases are before US courts; so...
  - → US law has the fair use principle
  - → US law does not have *sui generis* right on databases

- everything depends on **two fundamental questions**:
  - → is the training activity "transformative" enough to be covered by fair use?
  - → is it possible to concretely demonstrate the violation?

5. The prompt: what is its function and level of copyright protection?

As we have already briefly mentioned when talking about the Chinese case Li vs Liu (Beijing Internet Court), the decisions of the judges on the protectability of works created with generative artificial intelligence systems have recognized the importance of the role of prompts. This also in effect constitutes an unprecedented issue for copyright, which blurs the conventional boundaries of the concepts of creativity and authorship.

First of all, to avoid misunderstandings, let's define what it is: the prompt is the textual instruction that guides AI systems in generating content; and it is generally provided by the human user. The question (more philosophical-ontological than legal) that many ask is: does providing these textual instructions represent a creative act in all respects? And above all, is it sufficient to attribute to the user of the AI system the role of author and therefore of owner of the rights on the work thus generated?

According to some, prompt formulation today represents a new form of creative expression, in which human ingenuity manifests itself through the ability to construct precise, evocative and strategically structured instructions. This activity requires specific skills and an artistic vision that, although mediated by technology, maintains a significant authorial component.

In the context of the "new artificial creativity" therefore the author increasingly takes on the role of "creative director" or "conceptual architect" rather than material executor of the work. His function focuses on the definition of objectives, stylistic orientation and iterative refinement of prompts, delegating the technical execution of the content to artificial intelligence[13].

The current regulatory framework, conceived for a world still far from generative AI, shows clear limits in addressing these new creative dynamics.

---

13 Some artists use prompts as a form of creative writing, exploring the potential and limits of generative AI. For more on this topic see Alessandra Navazio, *Il prompt come scrittura creativa*, 26 January 2025, https://mangrovia.info/prompt-arte-intelligenza-artificiale/.

Copyright law will necessarily have to evolve to adequately recognize and protect the value of prompt engineering as an autonomous creative activity, establishing criteria of originality and worthy of protection. Simultaneously, developing authorship attribution models that recognize the collaborative nature of the human-machine creative process will be essential, moving beyond the traditional author-tool dichotomy.

In this perspective, we could argue that the prompt constitutes a form of intellectual work worthy of legal protection, as it represents the generative seed from which the final result springs and the human act in which the creative choices (the famous "judgement") are expressed to obtain the desired work; and as already in the prompt we can find the sum of the creative choices made by the author.

Gualtiero Dragotti makes a detailed argument[14], arriving at the conclusion that in fact, under certain conditions, the prompt itself can be considered protectable and making an interesting parallel with the protection of software.

> «These are works attributable to the creativity and personality of their author, which have an economic value and are easily reproducible. Admitting prompts to copyright protection, however, entails, in our system, some important corollaries. The first concerns the level of creativity of the work, which must exceed a minimum threshold, however low. The second concerns the extension of protection, which can never allow the author to monopolize technical solutions and devices,

14 Gualtiero Dragotti, *Generative AI and prompt protection under intellectual property law*, 2025, https://www.dlapiper.com/en-us/insights/publications/law-in-tech/generative-ai-and-prompt-protection-under-intellectual-property-law.

> which must remain available to everyone. Protection must therefore in principle be shaped along the lines of that provided for computer programs, which has as its object the external form of the work and not the ideas and technical solutions that determine its functioning.»

There is then a further aspect of the issue to consider: in some generative AI services there are "prepackaged" prompts, which the "lazier" or less familiar users with the tool can simply choose and "launch". Would there be protection in that case? And if so, whose rights would they be?

Perhaps we find an answer in the words of the American Copyright Office (USCO) which has had the opportunity to deal with the topic of prompting with precision and lucidity:

> «The Office concludes that, given current generally available technology, prompts alone do not provide sufficient human control to make users of an AI system the authors of the output. Prompts essentially function as instructions that convey unprotectible ideas. While highly detailed prompts could contain the user's desired expressive elements, at present they do not control how the AI system processes them in generating the output.
>
> Cases regarding joint authorship support this conclusion. These cases address the amount of control that is necessary to claim authorship. The provision of detailed directions, without influence over how those directions are executed, is insufficient.
>
> As the Third Circuit explained, when a person hires someone to execute their expression, "that process must be rote or mechanical transcription that does not require intellectual modification or highly technical enhancement" for the delegating party to claim copyright authorship in the final work.

Although entering prompts into a generative AI system can be seen as similar to providing instructions to an artist commissioned to create a work, there are key differences. In a human-to-human collaboration, the hiring party is able to oversee, direct, and understand the contributions of a commissioned human artist. Depending on the nature of each party's contributions, the artist may be the sole author, or the outcome may be a joint work or work for hire. In theory, AI systems could someday allow users to exert so much control over how their expression is reflected in an output that the system's contribution would become rote or mechanical. The evidence as to the operation of today's AI systems indicates that this is not currently the case. Prompts do not appear to adequately determine the expressive elements produced, or control how the system translates them into an output.»

6. The main short circuit: the similarity of outputs

In this whole scenario that now seems to have more defined contours we must consider a component capable of creating quite a bit of disorientation as it poses a new problem for copyright: the similarity of works generated with artificial intelligence.

The concept of creativity, as we framed it in the first chapter (comprising originality and novelty) has evolved and become established based on human creative methods and processes. In the "old world" if two creative works were very similar to each other it could be for two reasons. In the first hypothesis, the most probable and frequent, an author had plagiarized a pre-existing work, or both authors had plagiarized a pre-existing work; on this there is extensive case law that establishes how to handle these cases. In the second, much rarer, hypothesis, the authors by a bizarre twist of fate found themselves having the exact same creative inspiration and expressing it in a very similar way, however without one knowing the other's work.

With the spread of generative artificial intelligence platforms and with a new approach to copyright born from this revolution, the case of chance encounters may no longer be so rare. Because, as the OpenAI terms of use explain very clearly (which we will have the opportunity to comment on in more detail in the next chapter), this is intrinsic to the functioning of these technologies:

> «Due to the nature of our Services and artificial intelligence generally, output may not be unique and other users may receive similar output from our Services.»

Why do I talk about a "short circuit"? Because in fact the two users (let's call them John and Dick) who used an AI system by providing a similar input and therefore obtaining an equally similar output are unaware of what the other has done; nevertheless, they are both convinced that they hold exclusive rights because the platform's terms of use themselves give them such ownership. But at the same time, both John and Dick were warned by the terms of use themselves that this could happen; but most likely neither one nor the other have actually read and understood the terms of use, limiting themselves to "blindly accepting them" as a good part of users do.

Also on this aspect, it will be interesting to see how the judges will handle any disputes that will probably arise when the world of cultural production and communication begins to make assiduous use of these systems.

What is certain is that this "short circuit" also confirms the reflections that we have already proposed in the first chapter regarding the need to review the concept of creativity and protection of authorship from the ground up.

In the first edition of this book, I dedicated a few paragraphs to an experiment on the risk of similarity of outputs, particularly regarding images.

The experiment was conducted in May 2023 and consisted of launching two prompts composed of different words but which essentially asked for the exact same thing, that is, an image linked to a news story. I then involved a former PhD colleague of mine living in Malta and we synchronized to try to launch the prompts simultaneously on both Stable Diffusion and DALL-E to see if the results obtained could really be considered so similar as to create a risk of confusion.

Each of the platforms provided us with four images for each prompt to give a total of eight images, all with the same subject and the same style (indicated in the prompt), but all quite different. Overall, the characterization of the characters, the arrangement of the figures within the scene and the choice of settings and backgrounds seem sufficiently different to not suggest plagiarism. Even the fact that four outputs are provided for each input lowers the probability that the image chosen for publication by the first user is really similar to the one chosen by the second.

From this test (even if conducted without the claim of methodological solidity), it seems to have emerged that the risk of similarity of the content was not so marked.

Anyone who wants to see in detail the results obtained with this test is invited to view the previous edition of the book (available only in Italian version).

7. Towards a "hybrid" protection?

As mentioned earlier, Zarya of the Dawn was merely a pioneering case among many works created by human authors with significant support from generative artificial intelligence. This consequently prompted the USCO to establish a new practice in the registration of works and the attribution of rights. While machines or software cannot be considered co-authors, creative professionals now submit to the USCO works in which some parts stem from human ingenuity in the traditional sense, while for other parts humans primarily serve as prompt designers and "validators" of outputs.

According to some scholars, a form of hybrid copyright protection is consequently emerging; hybrid in that it considers both human and non-human contributions, assigning varying levels of protection to each element. The Zarya of the Dawn case has already applied a form of hybrid protection in which copyright protection was recognized for the skeleton of the work, the general concept, but not for the individual components of the work or the final mechanical output. The case involving author Elisa Shupe follows a similar pattern, who submitted a copyright request to the USCO for a novel written with the help of ChatGPT (titled "AI Machinations: Tangled Webs and Typed Words"). The USCO acknowledged her authorship not of the entire text, but only of the "selection, coordination and arrangement of the text generated by artificial intelligence"[15]. Among the theorists of this new form of hybrid protection, the most lucid is an Italian jurist, Alfredo Esposito, who had already anticipated this scenario in an article from March 2023[16] and identified the three key elements of "hybrid protection": i) protection of textual elements created by human beings; ii) recognition of creativity in the arrangement and selection; iii) exclusion of purely AI-generated components.

By February 2025, Esposito recognized that this theory had gained substantial maturity; and this occurs in the light of new cases similar to that of Zarya of the Dawn (such as the Rose Enigma case[17]) and after the publication of several official documents with which the USCO has publicly expressed its position on these cases:

> «While my 2023 analysis focused on the categorical exclusion of AI-generated elements, Rose Enigma demonstrates how the doctrine has evolved to recognize more subtle forms of human authorship. The earlier legal assessment suggested that "significant modification with a graphics processing program" could provide a pathway to copyright protection. The

15 In this regard, see Jim Mann, *How an American author tested the copyright laws for AI generated content*, 30 April 2024, https://lawdit.co.uk/readingroom/how-an-american-author-tested-the-copyright-laws-for-ai-generated-content.

16 See Alfredo Esposito, *Toward a hybrid copyright for AI-Generated works the U.S. Copyright Office decision*, 6 March 2023, https://www.alfredoesposito.eu/2023/03/06/toward-a-hybrid-copyright-for-ai-generated-works-the-u-s-copyright-office-decision/.

17 In this regard, see Atreya Mathur, *A Rose Enigma: Pending (Right) Protection*, 8 December 2023, https://itsartlaw.org/2023/12/08/rose-enigma/.

> Rose Enigma registration validates this interpretation while adding important nuances to the doctrine's practical application.»[1]

Esposito delves further, identifying three developments that in his opinion deserve particular attention:

> «First, the refinement of evaluation criteria for human contribution has moved beyond simple binary distinctions to embrace a more nuanced understanding of creative processes. This evolution reflects both technological advancement and deeper institutional understanding of AI-assisted creation.
>
> Second, the establishment of clear doctrinal guidelines for hybrid works provides creators with more certainty while maintaining necessary flexibility. The Rose Enigma case exemplifies how these guidelines can accommodate complex works that combine human creativity with AI assistance.
> Third, the preservation of fundamental copyright principles – particularly the requirement of human authorship – while adapting to technological change suggests a sustainable path forward for copyright law in the AI era.»

This is also the case of the most recent case involving filmmaker Andrew John King, who obtained a USCO registration of an AI-generated video with AI-generated music based on AI-generated elements modified.

As the very interesting blog Chatgptiseatingtheworld.com explains,

1 Source: Alfredo Esposito, *The Evolution of Hybrid Copyright: A Legal Analysis of AI-Generated Works from Zarya to Rose Enigma (2023-2025)*, 6 February 2025, https://www.alfredoesposito.eu/2025/02/06/hybrid-copyrigh-from-zarya-of-the-dawn-to-rose-enigma/.

«King wrote the lyrics for the song, with the music AI-generated, and then apparently edited a video he AI-generated with the music. Presumably, the editing of the video consists of King's selecting, coordinating, or arranging the AI-generated music and video elements, along with King's original lyrics. The copyright extends to that particular selection or arrangement, along with King's lyrics, but, the AI-generated elements are excluded from copyright. In other words, the video is a selection and arrangement of (1) copyrightable elements (lyrics) and (2) uncopyrightable elements (AI-generated music and video elements), and the particular selection and arrangement is itself copyrightable.»

Chapter 6 – What do the terms of service of the main platforms say about intellectual property?

1. Introduction

Generative AI systems are offered to users through two main distribution methods, each characterized by distinct legal and practical implications. These methods represent not only different technical approaches, but also different paradigms of relationship between providers and users, with consequent repercussions on the rights and obligations of both parties.

The first method consists of the offer of generative AI systems in the form of online services accessible via the web. In this scenario, the user interacts with the system through remote interfaces, while the computational infrastructure and the models remain under the direct control of the provider. The legal relationship between the parties is governed by terms of service, typically structured as an IT services contract. This configuration implies that the user never acquires ownership of the software, but only obtains a right of access conditional upon acceptance and compliance with the conditions unilaterally imposed by the provider, who retains broad discretion in modifying the terms and can suspend the service.

The second method consists of the distribution of AI software that can be installed directly on the user's machines. In this case, the AI system operates locally under the direct control of the user, albeit within the limits established by the license. The legal framework is configured as a traditional software license agreement, where the user acquires certain rights on the product without the supplier retaining direct control over its use. This configuration potentially offers greater autonomy, privacy and continuity of use, but also requires adequate technical skills and computational resources.

The significant differences between these two approaches are reflected in crucial aspects such as the protection of personal data, responsibility for the generated outputs, continuity of service and accessibility of features. While centralized online services facilitate continuous updates and require fewer user-side resources, installable systems guarantee greater independence and potentially fewer constraints in the processing of sensitive or controversial content, configuring themselves as complementary choices that respond to different needs and priorities of users.

Throughout this book, we have extensively referenced the terms of service of the main generative artificial intelligence platforms, since they are undoubtedly a sort of secondary "source of law" that cannot be ignored when venturing into frontier issues such as these and where the most concrete and direct answers to emerging legal problems are often found.

In this chapter, therefore, we will briefly present and comment on the terms of service and licenses of the main generative artificial intelligence systems. We will focus only on the parts dedicated to the topic of intellectual property; obviously, the commented documents are longer and more complex than the extracts you find here. Therefore, readers are advised not to rely solely on the information presented here and to consult the original documents.

In any case, before going into the merits of the individual AI services, let's make a theoretical introduction to correctly frame terms of service and licenses from a legal point of view.

2. Terms of online services: general framework

Let's first try to better understand what the terms of use are, how they are framed by legal theory and above all how they should be read and interpreted.

2.1. An agreement between the service provider and the user

Let's therefore understand what terms of use are and what type of regulatory document they constitute under law. The use of all online services, from the most established (such as YouTube, Facebook or Instagram) to the most recent (such as AI systems accessible via the web), is regulated by a contract that is established between the service provider and the user. This document is commonly called in English Terms of use, Terms of service (also abbreviated to TOS) or Terms and Conditions (also abbreviated to T&Cs) and is in all respects a contract that is prepared by the service provider and displayed on the website or in a specific section of the mobile application. We will use TOS for brevity.

According to the typical categories of civil law, it is therefore a bilateral contract (in the sense that it provides for reciprocal performances for both parties), standardized (because its content is always the same for all contracting parties) and a contract of adhesion (meaning one of the two parties can only adhere to the conditions as they are, without the possibility of proposing adjustments or modifications). It follows that, in fact, the text of these contracts is drafted by the legal office of the service provider and is displayed on the website or in the application so that it is easily viewable by all potential users; and the latter "sign" it when they register on the platform and check the appropriate box "I accept the terms of service". The fact that no one actually reads them and everyone accepts them almost without thinking is another matter. Furthermore, the TOS are periodically updated unilaterally by the service provider, and notification of these updates is sent to all users, with the warning that if the user does not agree with the changes made, they must cease using the service, and continued use will be understood as tacit acceptance.

This is a contract not standardized by law, so its form and structure must not be subject to particular constraints; what matters is that the obligations of the parties are made clear and unambiguous. Nonetheless, over the years, contractual practice has developed fairly standardized models, with clauses that are now difficult not to find in the TOS. Among these clauses we have: the definitions of key concepts for understanding the contract; the description of the service offered and how it works; the obligations of the parties relating to the use of the platform (permitted and non-permitted behaviors) and the resulting sanctions; the obligations regarding security and protection of personal data; the methods of managing intellectual property of the data and content created by the service provider and of those uploaded to the platform by the user; limitations of liability and various indemnities; any rules for managing payments and refunds (only for paid services); indication of the applicable legislation and the competent court in the event of disputes.

In addition to the actual TOS, some services prepare other non-mandatory documents that are intended to further clarify the legal aspects related to the use of the service and that, depending on the case, can be classified as policies (classic example: the copyright policy), user guidelines, or community standards. These are essentially parallel documents that are mentioned/referred to in the TOS; although they are not technically an integral part of the contract, they serve to clarify the contractual intention, to help the interpreter to understand and correctly apply the TOS and to more easily verify the lawfulness of the behaviors that occurred on the platform.

2.2. An additional layer of rules

The TOS try to regulate the various situations and legally relevant scenarios that can occur when using the platform; they establish which behaviors and contents are permitted and which are prohibited.

All of this, obviously, with a veiled tendency to protect the service provider and to discharge responsibility in their favor. After all, what else could we expect? They set up the platform, they maintain the servers, they pay the lawyers, and what's more, they let us use the service for free. In fact, let's keep in mind that the service provider is normally a commercial entity, which must do business and generate revenue, making the most of the huge investments made and protecting itself as much as possible from legal risks that could damage it.

We can therefore say that the TOS, in a certain sense, represent an "additional layer of rules" of a contractual nature; a layer that in many cases becomes the first point of reference to look at in the event of problems and disputes. Is someone violating my privacy by publishing an image without my consent, or infringing my copyright by using my music without a legitimate license? Before even contacting a lawyer or the competent authorities, I can try to leverage the internal rules of the platform and ask the service provider to intervene.

Moreover, as we have already explained in the first chapter, we find ourselves in a world in which innovation is moving at a truly impressive speed and the law is seriously struggling to keep up. And so it often happens that, even before the judges with their sentences, the first to provide concrete answers to the new challenges of the law are precisely the legal departments of the companies that develop innovative technologies. This is why in the end it becomes central and interesting to turn our gaze to the legal departments of the companies engaged in the challenges of technological innovation and look for the first answers precisely in the TOS that they have drafted and made available. All this is particularly true in the case we are dealing with, generative artificial intelligence: a disruptive innovation like few others, which from a legal point of view raises questions that are not easy to solve and for which, at the moment, there are not many solid answers.

2.3. The "psychological" aspect

In all this, we must also consider a – so to speak – psychological aspect that could also be considered as a form of "legal neurosis": the vast majority of users of web platforms and smartphone applications have never read a single line of the TOS, despite having accepted them when first registering and having accepted them again with each update notification. If you find yourself in front of an audience of teenagers, try asking everyone who has an Instagram account to raise their hand and you will see a mass of almost unanimous raised hands. Then ask only those who have read the TOS at least once or even those who have asked their parents to read the TOS for them to raise their hand, and you will see a desert.

We all do it, there's no point in denying it; even those like me who, by their mindset, should be more inclined to read that type of documents do it. Time is short, laziness is a very common sin, we often lack the skills to understand certain terms, texts are often intentionally long and written in a bureaucratic style (with all due respect to emerging theories on legal design)... But above all, why should I read the terms of service and have doubts about the legal implications of a certain service, if deep down I have already decided that I want to use that service? I think this is the real question.

Furthermore, since these are – as we have explained – membership contracts, whose text is standard and established by the service provider and in which there would be no room for negotiation anyway, the user would only have the choice of not joining, of staying out of the game.

But never! The rush to keep up with the various available technologies, what in psychological terms is called FOMO (i.e. fear of missing out) leads us to always have to be part of the game; and to be part of the game we must accept the rules of the game, written and updated by the one who organized the championship and who also owns the playing fields.

It is a mechanism that has been with us for almost twenty years now and to which we are now quite accustomed; but if we look closely it signals a general lack of legal awareness among a good part of users, which dangerously adds to a very low awareness also on the technical IT level.

Even the advent of generative artificial intelligence platforms is not immune to these dynamics. The following paragraphs should contribute to at least partially increasing the level of awareness, although limited to the aspect of intellectual property management.

3. Licenses of AI software that can be installed on user's devices

As we have already written, some artificial intelligence systems are distributed as applications that can be installed by users on their machines. Users come into possession of the installable packages upon acceptance of the conditions of a license, i.e. a document with which the owner of the rights to the software communicates to users which authorizations are granted and which conditions are set out. Let's focus on some basic concepts on software licenses and then make some specific considerations on licenses for the use of generative artificial intelligence software.

3.1. Copyright licenses in general

Software licenses are a type of contract that obviously arrived relatively recently (70s/80s), but are now quite rooted and standardized. To understand what a license is, let's start with the etymological analysis of the term: the word "license" comes from the Latin "licere", which means "to allow", and generally indicates an authorization act, a permission given.

The rights holder (licensor) grants the user (licensee) the ability to make certain uses of the work, provided the latter adheres to certain conditions. The license to use therefore represents a conditional permission, a sort of "you can do X on condition that you do Y". We can in fact say that licenses always have "two souls": a part in which the uses granted are indicated and another part in which the conditions that the user must respect are indicated.

From the perspective of Italian legal theory, the license to use intellectual works is an atypical contract (i.e. not governed by specific legal rules) and is commonly associated with the rental agreement. Sticking to this metaphor, we can think of a work of the mind as an apartment that is rented. In the metaphor, the owner of the apartment is the owner of the rights to the work (which depending on the case can be a publishing house, a record company, a software house, or even the author himself); the tenant is instead the user and licensee of the work; the rental contract is precisely the license to use.

Consider the case of a law firm that needs a database with laws and court rulings. On the one hand, we have the licenses aimed at a defined licensee: in this case the licensor Tizio offers the work under license to the licensee Caio. It is therefore a contract signed by two parties and structured to regulate their specific relationship. Let us think about the case of a law firm that needs a database with laws and sentences.

The firm will contact the publishing house that creates this database and ask for a license to use the work. The publishing house will tend to propose a license agreement specifically for the firm's needs, which will take into account various factors, such as the number of professionals working in the firm, the license duration, and the types of content included in the database (only laws, only court rulings, both, etc.). This is therefore the case that most closely fits the metaphor of the rental agreement for an apartment just mentioned.

On the other hand, there are licenses in which only the licensor is a specific subject, while the licensee is undefined; any user who decides to use the work on the basis of the authorizations and conditions indicated in the license becomes a licensee. These are therefore public and standardized licenses. Let's take the case of purchasing a computer, one of those with an integrated operating system; once the device is purchased, upon first startup, the buyer will see a standard license, the same for any user; the buyer can only accept it as it is, or even reject it (but in that case they would be required not to use that copy of the operating system). As another example, let's think about the case of open licenses, that is, licenses for open source software and licenses for open content (Creative Commons and similar), which, despite having a handful of variants, represent standard documents known throughout the world.

3.2. Open licenses

The licenses that belong to the category just mentioned share common characteristics with so-called contracts of adhesion, and acceptance by the user/licensee occurs through conclusive behavior; that is, the simple fact of using the work implies its use in compliance with the conditions imposed by the license. Failure to comply with these conditions automatically causes the permissions granted by the license to lapse.

Always using metaphorical language, we can also distinguish licenses based on their level of "openness". An open license is one in which the freedoms granted to users prevail in both quantity and scope over the imposed conditions. In a certain sense, the rights holder applies an open license to his works to reopen what the "closed by default" principle of copyright has kept closed. On the contrary, a proprietary license is a license in which the conditions imposed prevail over the permissions granted to users. By applying these licenses, the rights holder does nothing but emphasize and further strengthen the limitations imposed by copyright and in some cases add new and more specific ones.

The best-known licenses belonging to the category of open licenses for software are those drawn up by the GNU Project, such as the GNU GPL and the GNU LGPL in their various versions, which still represent the most widely used licenses in the world for free and open source software. For other types of works (non-software), however, the licenses that have now been established as a sort of reference standard for twenty years are the Creative Commons licenses.

A well-known generative AI service for images, Midjourney, mentioned Creative Commons licenses in the first version of its terms of use; the document has now been updated and modified, but it was the subject of specific commentary in the first version of this book (only Italian).

3.3. Main generative AI systems that can be installed on your devices: Stable Diffusion and Flux

Based on what has been illustrated in these last two paragraphs, we are now able to better understand what it means (from a legal point of view) to use a generative AI system that can be installed on your device.

It is a choice that, compared to that of using an AI service via the web, undoubtedly allows the user greater control, both from a technical and legal point of view[2]. On a technical level, for example, it is possible to use some specific models while excluding others, choose the preferred user interface or even write one specifically. On a legal level, the data and queries are managed locally on your device and therefore you have full control of the inputs provided to the system (which can include texts, private documents, images,

2 For further insight, see Paolo Dalprato, *Licenze AI Generativa: guida essenziale per professionisti*, 2 September 2024, https://www.ai4business.it/intelligenza-artificiale/licenze-ai-generativa-guida-essenziale-per-professionisti/.

videos, and music), because they are never sent to a third party and never uploaded to a server located in some country that does not offer guarantees of protection of privacy and intellectual property.

The best known of the generative AI systems made available in an installable version is certainly Stable Diffusion; some online services for generating images, in fact, are based precisely on the Stable Diffusion models (such as Leonardo.ai, and Krea.ai).

On the StabilityAI website (the company that produces Stable Diffusion) we find two options for acquiring a license: a "Community" license which is free and aimed at users (individuals or companies) with an annual income of less than one million dollars; an "Enterprise" license aimed at large companies, with dedicated support and specific training of the models, with a price to be agreed upon.

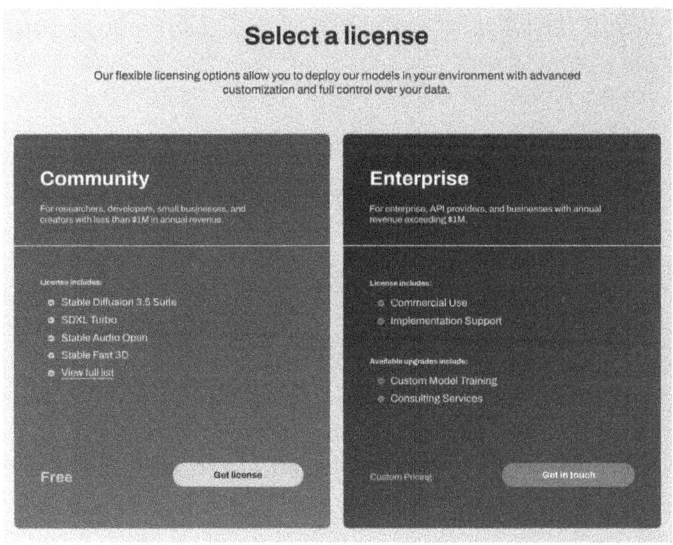

Figure 9: Screenshot of the StabilityAI website with the different

license options.

Let's now open the "Community" license[3] and focus on the part dedicated to the management of intellectual property rights, i.e. paragraph IV.c., which first talks about "Ownership of Derivative Works" (with a very unclear paragraph) and then about "Ownership of Outputs":

> «Ownership of Derivative Works. As between You and Stability AI, You are the owner of Derivative Works You create, subject to Stability AI's ownership of the Stability AI Materials and any Derivative Works made by or for Stability AI.
> Ownership of Outputs. As between You and Stability AI, You own any outputs generated from the Models or Derivative Works to the extent permitted by applicable law.»

According to the definitions provided at the end of the license, "Stability AI Materials" means collectively:

> «Stability's proprietary Models, Software and Documentation (and any portion or combination thereof) made available under this Agreement.»

While "Derivative Works" means:

> «(a) any derivative work of the Stability AI Materials as recognized by U.S. copyright laws and (b) any modifications to a Model, and any other model created which is based on or derived from the Model or the Model's output, including "fine tune" and "low-rank adaptation" models derived from a Model or a Model's output, but do not include the output of any Model.»

Other important and widespread generative artificial intelligence models that can be installed on user

3 The document is available at https://stability.ai/community-license-agreement.

devices are the Flux models created and distributed by Black Forest Labs (a company based in Delaware). They are divided into different categories: Flux.1 Schnell, designed for local development and personal use, available under the Apache 2.0 license and therefore classifiable as "open source"; Flux.1 Dev, designed for more advanced and professional use, but still non-commercial; Flux.1 Pro is designed for commercial and professional uses, and can be used after purchasing specific subscriptions.

There has been quite a bit of debate within the developer community about how to identify the distinction between commercial and non-commercial uses[4]. The answer can however be found in the "FLUX.1 [dev] Non-Commercial License"[5] which provides the definition of Non-Commercial Purpose in article 1.3.

> «"Non-Commercial Purpose" means any of the following uses, but only so far as you do not receive any direct or indirect payment arising from the use of the model or its output: (i) personal use for research, experiment, and testing for the benefit of public knowledge, personal study, private entertainment, hobby projects, or otherwise not directly or indirectly connected to any commercial activities, business operations, or employment responsibilities; (ii) use by commercial or for-profit entities for testing, evaluation, or non-commercial research and development in a non-production environment, (iii) use by any charitable organization for charitable purposes, or for testing or evaluation.

---

4 https://www.reddit.com/r/StableDiffusion/comments/1em68gt/yeah_flux1_is_great_but_what_about_license/.

5 The document is available at https://huggingface.co/black-forest-labs/FLUX.1-dev/blob/main/LICENSE.md.

> For clarity, use for revenue-generating activity or direct interactions with or impacts on end users, or use to train, fine tune or distill other models for commercial use is not a Non-Commercial purpose.»

The same license also provides us with the regulation on the rights of use on the outputs; more precisely, this occurs in article 2.4. entitled "Outputs", which states:

> «We claim no ownership rights in and to the Outputs. You are solely responsible for the Outputs you generate and their subsequent uses in accordance with this License. You may use Output for any purpose (including for commercial purposes), except as expressly prohibited herein. You may not use the Output to train, fine-tune or distill a model that is competitive with the FLUX.1 [dev] Model.»

4. The distinction between provider and deployer in the AI Act

In the context of the European Regulation on Artificial Intelligence (AI Act), the distinction between "provider" and "deployer" represents a key aspect for attributing responsibilities along the value chain of AI systems. This distinction precisely outlines the different roles and obligations of the actors involved in the development, commercialization and use of AI technologies in the European market.

The provider, according to Article 3, no. 3 of the AI Act, is defined as

> «a natural or legal person, public authority, agency or other body that develops an AI system or a gener-

> al-purpose AI model or that has an AI system or a general-purpose AI model developed and places it on the market or puts the AI system into service under its own name or trademark, whether for payment or free of charge.»

It is therefore the entity that designs, creates, and places the technology on the market, assuming responsibility for the system's compliance with the regulatory requirements set forth in the regulation.

The deployer, on the other hand, as established by Article 3, number 4 of the AI Act, is

> «a natural or legal person, public authority, agency or other body using an AI system under its authority except where the AI system is used in the course of a personal non-professional activity.»

It is therefore configured as the professional user of the system, who implements the technology in their operational processes and determines the specific methods of use.

The distinction is crucial because the regulation imposes differentiated obligations: while the supplier is primarily responsible for the intrinsic compliance of the system, the deployer must ensure its appropriate use in compliance with the indications provided and the specific obligations relating to the application context. This approach reflects the European legislator's desire to distribute responsibilities in a proportionate manner along the entire AI value chain, thus ensuring a balance between technological innovation and the protection of fundamental rights.

5. The OSI Open Source AI Definition

In the contemporary technological landscape, characterized by a rapid evolution of artificial intelligence systems, the need to define shared standards that can guide the development of accessible and transparent technologies is becoming increasingly pressing. In this context, the Open Source Initiative (OSI), an organization that has always been committed to promoting and protecting open source software, has recently developed the Open Source AI Definition (OSAID), a fundamental document that establishes the criteria necessary for an artificial intelligence system to be defined as authentically open source. This initiative represents an attempt to transfer the historical principles of the open source movement – transparency, accessibility, modifiability and sharing – into the domain of artificial intelligence, thus creating a conceptual and legal framework that can guide developers, researchers and end users. The document, in its essential clarity, states:

> «An Open Source AI is an AI system made available under terms and in a way that grant the freedoms to:
>
> - Use the system for any purpose and without having to ask for permission.
> - Study how the system works and inspect its components.
> - Modify the system for any purpose, including to change its output.
> - Share the system for others to use with or without modifications, for any purpose.
>
> These freedoms apply both to a fully functional system and to discrete elements of a system. A precondition to exercising these freedoms is to have access to the preferred form to make modifications to the system.»

This definition is a response to growing concerns about the concentration of technological power in the hands of a few commercial entities and the lack of transparency that characterizes many contemporary AI systems. By articulating these four fundamental freedoms – use, study, modify, and share – the OSI seeks to foster a more democratic AI ecosystem, where knowledge flows freely and barriers to access are minimized.

The emphasis on access to the "preferred form of modification" also highlights the importance of true technical accessibility, moving beyond superficial open source approaches that may be limited to simply publishing code without the tools needed to truly understand and modify systems.

6. The TOS of OpenAI

Let's start with OpenAI's TOS covering ChatGPT, DALL-E, Sora and the other services of the company led by Sam Altman. The document addresses the user with the second person, so "you", "they", "your" refer to the user. The topic of intellectual property on generated content is discussed in the paragraph entitled "Content". Let's look at the most salient passages in detail.

6.1. Management of rights on generated content

First of all, we proceed to a definition of "content" and talk about the distinction between "input" and "output": the first is the command provided by the user to the AI system (which can be a text, an image, or another type of file); the second is what the AI system creates starting from that input. We read:

> «You may provide input to the Services ("Input"), and receive output from the Services based on the Input ("Output"). Input and Output are collectively "Content". You are responsible for Content, including ensuring that it does not violate any applicable law or these Terms. You represent and warrant that you have all rights, licenses, and permissions needed to provide Input to our Services.»

The TOS also take the opportunity to clarify a fundamental aspect, that is, who should be held responsible for the input also in terms of intellectual property. In essence, by using OpenAI's services and uploading copyrighted works, the user declares that they have the necessary rights or authorizations and indirectly releases the service provider from any liability.

The paragraph immediately following moves on to the central aspect of ownership of usage rights:

> «As between you and OpenAI, and to the extent permitted by applicable law, you (a) retain your ownership rights in Input and (b) own the Output. We hereby assign to you all our right, title, and interest, if any, in and to Output.»

The approach therefore seems very clear: all rights belong to the user, both those on the inputs and those on the outputs and therefore on the works generated.

For its part, OpenAI reserves the right to use the contents for its own internal purposes:

> «We may use Content to provide, maintain, develop, and improve our Services, comply with applicable law,

enforce our terms and policies, and keep our Services safe.»

In any case, immediately after, OpenAI's TOS takes care of offering users the possibility of the so-called "opt-out" and reminding that, if a user does not want their contents to be used to train OpenAI models, there is the possibility to opt out, making this choice explicit in the account settings.

6.2. The problem of similarity of outputs

One of the most interesting aspects that emerge in OpenAI's TOS is that of "similarity of content", which has already been the subject of some general reflections in the previous chapter; now we can see more specifically how it is treated by OpenAI. In the following paragraph B, while assigning the user the rights to use the output, OpenAI warns us that, depending on the inputs entered, the system could provide a very similar or even identical result to two or more users:

> «Due to the nature of our Services and artificial intelligence generally, output may not be unique and other users may receive similar output from our Services. Our assignment above does not extend to other users' output or any Third Party Output.»

In essence, with the last sentence of this paragraph, OpenAI is absolving itself of any liability related to the similarity of outputs and potential intellectual property disputes between different users who, though unaware, have obtained very similar results. As if to say: "we warned you that it could happen, so don't blame us".

The question at this point becomes: can I perhaps blame the other user who, despite having arrived after me and being in good faith, obtained an output very similar or identical to mine and published it, thus spreading a work that can be confused with mine? A nice dilemma, given that, according to what OpenAI's TOS says, we both have full rights of use, albeit on things that are actually very similar or identical. Who can sue whom? There are no answers to this for now, and we will have to await specific case law. But as we have had the opportunity to explain in the previous chapter, it is not so likely that the outputs are so obviously similar as to be able to generate a lawsuit.

6.3. A look at the sharing policy and usage policy

In addition to the Terms of Service in the strict sense, the OpenAI website also displays another document of fundamental importance: the "sharing and publication policy"[6], that is the methods and indications that the OpenAI user should observe when spreading content generated with ChatGPT or DALL-E. This document also has a contractual value and the user declares to have read and accepted it at the time of registration; its main function is to release OpenAI from a series of responsibilities that may arise from the dissemination of the outputs (in the introduction it is in fact written "To mitigate the possible risks of AI-generated content, we have set the following policy on permitted sharing").

6 The document is available at https://openai.com/policies/sharing-publication-policy.

While specifying that in general it is permitted to publish the outputs obtained on social media, as well as broadcast live the use or make public demonstrations with OpenAI products, the service provider asks that the following conditions be respected:

> «Manually review each generation before sharing or while streaming.
> Attribute the content to your name or your company.
> Indicate that the content is AI-generated in a way no user could reasonably miss or misunderstand.
> Do not share content that violates our Content Policy or that may offend others.
> If taking audience requests for prompts, use good judgment; do not input prompts that might result in violations of our Content Policy.»

In the fourth point, therefore, reference is made to a further document entitled "Usage policies"[7] where it is defined which uses of the service are expressly prohibited.

Reading this document, there are no particular references to the scope of copyright, other than those to practices of "academic dishonesty".

7. The TOS of Midjourney

Now let's move on to the terms of use of Midjourney[8], another widely used platform specialized in the creation of artistic images.

The paragraph that interests us is paragraph 4, which is entitled "Rights to Content". First of all, in

7 The document is available at https://openai.com/policies/usage-policies/.

8 The document is available at https://docs.midjourney.com/docs/terms-of-service.

the sub-paragraph "Your Rights and Obligations", the user's rights of use on the content created with the service are clarified, first establishing a general principle of ownership of rights and then specifying some exceptions. Among these exceptions, the most interesting is the one that establishes a general distinction between "simple" users and large companies, that is, companies with an annual gross turnover of more than one million dollars. The latter, in order to own the created assets, must subscribe to a Pro subscription for each person who accesses the service.

> «You own all Assets You create with the Services to the fullest extent possible under applicable law. There are some exceptions:
> - Your ownership is subject to any obligations imposed by this Agreement and the rights of any third-parties.
> - If you are a company or any employee of a company with more than $1,000,000 USD a year in revenue, you must be subscribed to a "Pro" or "Mega" plan to own Your Assets.
> - If you upscale the images of others, these images remain owned by the original creators. [...]»

Midjourney therefore also uses the million-dollar parameter to differentiate between users and their licenses:

> «Inputs, Assets, and other content such as messages, photos, videos, and documents that you may provide to the Services (such as through uploading, posting, sharing, or chat messages) are collectively, "Content". You are responsible for all Content that you provide or generate, including ensuring that it does not violate any applicable laws or this Agreement, and that you

> have all necessary rights and permissions to provide the Content.»

From a clearly synallagmatic perspective, on the one hand, it establishes what rights the service provider grants to the user regarding the outputs; on the other, it clarifies what rights the user grants to the service provider regarding the inputs inserted into the AI system. This is stated in the following paragraph "Rights you grant to Midjourney":

> «By using the Services, You grant to Midjourney, its affiliates, successors, and assigns a perpetual, worldwide, non-exclusive, sublicensable no-charge, royalty-free, irrevocable copyright license to reproduce, prepare derivative works of, publicly display, publicly perform, sublicense, and distribute the Content You input into the Services, as well as any Assets produced by You through the Service. This license survives termination of this Agreement by any party, for any reason.»

These clauses follow a fairly standard model that is also largely found in the terms of use of content sharing platforms (Facebook, YouTube, Instagram and the like), through which the service provider obtains a wide range of freedom of use over content uploaded by users.

As we have already mentioned, in a previous version of the terms of use (the one from Spring 2023 that we discussed in the first edition of this book), the application of a Creative Commons license was also foreseen; a reference that no longer appears.

Shortly after, the Midjourney TOS adds a note that is intended to warn the user in less "legalese" terms of the implications of what is written in the previous paragraphs (and in a certain sense to recommend the purchase of a Pro plan to have fewer worries):

> «Please note: Midjourney is an open community which allows others to use and remix Your Content whenever they are posted in a public setting. By default, Your Content is publically viewable and remixable. As described below, You grant Midjourney a license to allow this.»

Let's now move on to paragraph 5 entitled "DMCA Policy and Removal" and dedicated precisely to the policies for the removal of content that violates copyright (according to the principles of the Digital Millennium Copyright Act, a US law of 1998).

In essence, as occurs in all content sharing platforms regulated by US law, the service provider indicates the procedures to follow in the event that someone browsing the platform finds content that violates their copyright or related rights and that has therefore been uploaded without authorization (circumventing any automated controls of the platform itself).

8. The TOS of Claude.ai

The TOS of Claude.ai[9] (an AI platform created by the American company Anthropic) address the issue of intellectual property with particular attention to user responsibility and the ownership of generated content. First of all, it is emphasized that users remain fully responsible for the "Input" provided to the system, having to guarantee that they have the necessary rights for its use. This means that anyone

9 The document is available at https://www.anthropic.com/legal/consumer-terms.

who enters text, images or other data into Claude.ai services must ensure that they do not violate third-party rights, such as patents, copyrights or privacy laws. This is expressed in Article 3 entitled "Use of our Services":

> «You are responsible for all activity under the account through which you access the Services. You may not access or use, or help another person to access or use, our Services in the following ways: [...]
>
> 6) to infringe, misappropriate, or violate intellectual property or other legal rights (including the rights of publicity or privacy).»

The following article 4 ("Input, output and materials") moves to the central aspect of our analysis, that is, the rights of use on inputs and outputs. First of all, the definitions are clarified:

> «You may be allowed to interact with our Services in a variety of formats (we call these "Inputs"). Our Services may generate responses (we call these "Outputs") or enable the Services to take actions on your behalf, such as software manipulation, data processing, and system interactions (we call these "Actions"), based on your Inputs. Inputs and Outputs collectively are "Materials".»

Subsequently, in the subsection "Rights on Materials", the responsibilities on inputs and the rights of use on outputs are established:

> «You are responsible for all Inputs you submit to our Services and all Actions. You must ensure that you have all rights, licenses, and permissions that are necessary for us to process such Inputs in accordance with our Terms and to provide the Services to you, including for example, to integrate with third-party services, to share Materials with others at your direction, and to

> take Actions. You must ensure that your submission of Inputs to us, your sharing them with others, or directing Claude to take Actions will not violate our Terms, our Acceptable Use Policy, or any laws or regulations applicable to those Inputs. As between you and Anthropic, and to the extent permitted by applicable law, you retain any right, title, and interest that you have in such Inputs. Subject to your compliance with our Terms, we assign to you all our right, title, and interest (if any) in Outputs.»

But what does Anthropic do with the input provided by users? The answer is in another subsection of Section 4 of the TOS:

> «We may use Materials to provide, maintain, and improve the Services and to develop other products and services. We will not train our models on any Materials that are not publicly available, except in two circumstances:
> If you provide Feedback to us (through the Services or otherwise) regarding any Materials, we may use that Feedback in accordance with Section 5 (Feedback).
> If your Materials are flagged for trust and safety review, we may use or analyze those Materials to improve our ability to detect and enforce Acceptable Use Policy violations, including training models for use by our trust and safety team, consistent with Anthropic's safety mission.»

9. The TOS of Leonardo.ai

Among the widely used generative AI services, there is one that has TOS that are quite different from the fairly standard and aligned texts that we have commented on so far: Leonardo AI[10]. The governing law and jurisdiction for these TOS are Australian, more precisely, those of New South Wales.

Leonardo.ai implements the Stable Diffusion models in a platform that is particularly high-performance in image generation, which has a fairly large and active user base.

The part of the TOS that concerns the management of intellectual property is paragraph 8 entitled "Ownership of inputs and outputs"; as we have already seen in other TOS, inputs and outputs are collectively defined as "Content".

Paragraph 8.2 clarifies the responsibilities for Inputs and ownership of them:

> «You are responsible for all Inputs you submit to our Services. By submitting Inputs to our Service, you represent, warrant and agree that you have all rights, licenses and permissions necessary for us to use and process the Inputs and to generate Outputs. You retain ownership of any Inputs.»

The next paragraph 8.3 moves on to the aspect of ownership of the Outputs; and it is here that the different approach chosen by Leonardo emerges. In fact, a distinction is drawn between paying users (who have signed up for a subscription) and non-paying users (who use the free version of the platform). Paying users are recognized as having intellectual property rights over the generated content, while non-paying users receive different treatment:

> «If you are on one of our paid Subscriptions [...] ownership of all Intellectual Property Rights in any Content

10 The document is available at https://leonardo.ai/terms-of-service/.

> you, or your Authorised Users, create while using the Platform will vest in you upon creation, and to the extent that ownership of such Intellectual Property Rights does not automatically vest in you, we hereby assign all such Intellectual Property Rights to you and agree to do all other things necessary to assure your title in such rights.»

This is also mirrored in paragraph 8.7, which highlights that, in the case of non-paying users, the intellectual property rights are instead transferred to Leonardo.ai:

> «If you are on one of our free Subscriptions [...], ownership of all Intellectual Property Rights in any Output you, or your Authorised Users, create while using the Platform will vest in us upon creation, and to the extent that ownership of such Intellectual Property Rights does not automatically vest in us, you hereby assign all such Intellectual Property Rights to us and agree to do all other things necessary to assure our title in such rights.»

In paragraph 8.4, a further distinction is drawn: that between Public Content and Private Content, with the respective legal consequences. And it is the paying users who can choose which of these two categories the generated content should fall into:

> «Certain Paid Subscribers can select whether Content is public or private. You acknowledge and agree that Content marked public (Public Content) will be available for use by all users on the Platform. Where you opt for Content to be private (Private Content), only you and your Authorised Users can access that Content. [...]»

Lastly, a final critical comment can be found in paragraph 8.8. dedicated to the delicate aspect of moral rights:

> «If you [...] or any of your personnel have any Moral Rights in any material provided, used or prepared in connection with these Terms, you agree to (and will procure that your personnel) consent to our use or infringement of those Moral Rights.»

Although Australian law deals with the issue of moral rights with a particular approach compared to other jurisdictions, it sounds truly bizarre to find in a contractual act (such as the terms of service of these online platforms) a clause for the management of author's moral rights. According to European law, moral rights are in fact personal rights and as such they are exquisitely unavailable, non-transferable, inalienable; this means that the author cannot in any case dispose of them by contract nor renounce their exercise by contract. Even less sensible seems the commitment to authorize a priori a violation of such rights and the fact that the user can dispose of moral rights of a member of his staff. This passage therefore remains quite controversial.

10. The TOS of Deepseek

Given the disruptive success achieved since its first days, we cannot fail to dedicate a few words to the TOS of Deepseek[11], an online generative AI platform of Chinese origin obviously governed by the law of the People's Republic of China, with jurisdiction set in Hangzhou (the Chinese city where the company is based).

11 The document is available at https://cdn.deepseek.com/policies/en-US/deepseek-terms-of-use.html.

Regardless of the legislation and jurisdiction applied, the model followed by Deepseek TOS for the management of intellectual property is fairly standard and aligned with most similar platforms.

First of all, in paragraph 3.6, among the commitments that the user must assume by using the platform, there is that of not violating the intellectual property rights of third parties and therefore not using creative works protected by copyright or protected trademarks as input:

> «You will not use the Services for the following improper purposes: [...]
> Engaging in activities that infringe on intellectual property rights, trade secrets, and other violations of business ethics, or using algorithms, data, platforms, etc., to implement monopolistic and unfair competition behaviors.»

However, it is paragraph 4 (titled "Inputs and Outputs") that is more central to our analysis. In subparagraph 4.1, the obligation previously mentioned in paragraph 3.6 is reiterated:

> «You are responsible for all Inputs you submit to our Services and corresponding Outputs. By submitting Inputs to our Services, you represent and warrant that you have all rights, licenses, and permissions that are necessary for us to process the Inputs under our Terms. You also represent and warrant that your submitting Inputs to us and corresponding Outputs will not violate our Terms, or any laws or regulations applicable to those Inputs and Outputs.»

The following subparagraph 4.2 clarifies the ownership of the rights to the generated content:

> «[...] you have the following rights regarding the Inputs and Outputs of the Services: (1) You retain any rights, title, and interests—if any—in the Inputs you submit; (2) We assign any rights, title, and interests—if any—in the Outputs of the Services to you. (3) You may apply the Inputs and Outputs of the Services to a wide range of use cases, including personal use, academic research, derivative product development, training other models (such as model distillation), etc.»

Since its launch to the general public (at the end of January 2025), Deepseek has been announced as an open source generative AI system. In reality, more precisely, on the project's Github repository[1], there are two licenses: an MIT license[2] (which is in fact classified as an open source license by the Open Source Initiative) and a license drafted by Deepseek and not classifiable as open source.

However, it is not clear to which components the two licenses apply respectively. According to what is explained on the repository itself in paragraph 7, all the computer code is made available to the public under the MIT license (indicated as "Code License"); the other license (indicated as "Model license") governs the use of the DeepSeek-V3 Base/Chat models and therefore represents more of a terms of service than a software license in the strict sense.

1 See https://github.com/deepseek-ai/.

2 More information about the license are available at the related Wikipedia entry (https://en.wikipedia.org/wiki/MIT_License).

APPENDIX – Synthetic and schematic analysis of the most interesting judicial cases

(original version by Paolo Dalprato[3]; English translation by Simone Aliprandi)

A – Thaler vs Perlmutter/USCO (U.S. District Court for the District of Columbia, USA, 2023)

A.1 – Points analyzed by the Court

The court examined the following key points to reach its decision.

1. Interpretation of the term "author" in copyright law:

- The court analyzed the meaning of the term "author" in the context of copyright law.
- It concluded that, although not explicitly defined in the law, the term "author" implies a human creator.

2. Historical analysis of the concept of authorship:

3 The original version of this appendix was published in the Italian book *Creatività ibrida. Autore e opera nell'era delle macchine intelligenti* written by Paolo Dalprato and published by Ledizioni in March 2025 under a Creative Commons BY-SA 4.0 license; full details on the book here: https://www.ledizioni.it/prodotto/creativita-ibrida/.

- The court examined the legislative and jurisprudential history of copyright in the United States.
- It highlighted that the original intent of copyright law was to incentivize human creativity.

3. Assessment of AI's role in the creative process:
- The court considered AI's role as a tool, rather than as an author.
- It established that the use of advanced technological tools does not preclude copyright protection, but still requires significant human creative intervention.

4. Examination of legal precedents:
- The court analyzed previous cases involving works created without direct human intervention (such as alleged divine communications or photographs taken by animals).
- It concluded that these precedents support the requirement of human authorship.

5. Considerations on future implications:
- The court recognized the future challenges posed by the increasing use of AI in artistic creation.
- It suggested the need for further discussions and possible legislative adjustments to address these challenges.

A.2 – Timeline of actions taken by Thaler

1. Creation of the work:
- Thaler used his AI system called "Creativity Machine" to generate the visual artwork "A Recent Entrance to Paradise".

- The work was created autonomously by the AI system without direct human intervention in the creative process.

2. Copyright registration application:
- Thaler submitted a copyright registration application to the United States Copyright Office.
- In the application, he listed the "Creativity Machine" as the author of the work.
- He requested to be registered as the copyright owner as the owner of the machine.

3. First refusal by the Copyright Office:
- The Copyright Office denied registration, stating that the work lacked the human authorship necessary for copyright protection.

4. First request for reconsideration:
- Thaler requested reconsideration of the decision.
- He confirmed that the work had been generated autonomously by AI and lacked traditional human authorship.
- He challenged the Copyright Office's human authorship requirement.

5. Second refusal by the Copyright Office:
- The Copyright Office confirmed the refusal, reiterating that copyright law is limited to "original intellectual conceptions of the author".

6. Second request for reconsideration:
- Thaler submitted a second request for reconsideration.

7. Final refusal by the Copyright Review Board:
- The Copyright Review Board confirmed the refusal of registration.

8. Legal action:
- Thaler filed a lawsuit against the Copyright Office in the United States District Court for the District of Columbia.
- He argued that the refusal of registration violated the Administrative Procedure Act.

9. Court decision:
- The court examined the case and issued a ruling in favor of the Copyright Office.
- It confirmed that United States copyright law requires human authorship and that works generated autonomously by AI are not copyrightable.

A.3 – Key Court considerations

1. Interpretation of the law:
- The court emphasized that the requirement of human authorship is implicit in the text of copyright law and its legislative history.

2. Adaptability of copyright:
- It recognized that copyright has adapted over time to include new forms of creative expression, but has always maintained the requirement of human intervention.

3. Role of AI:
- It clarified that AI can be used as a tool in the creative process, but cannot be considered an "author" under copyright law.

4. Future challenges:
- It recognized that the increasing use of AI in artistic creation will pose new challenges to copyright law, suggesting the need for further discussions and possible legislative adjustments.

5. Limitations of the decision:
- The Court emphasized that the decision applies specifically to cases where AI generates works completely autonomously, without significant human intervention.

This detailed analysis of the Thaler vs. Copyright Office case offers an in-depth view of the legal and creative complexities involved in creating works with the aid of generative AI, providing an important precedent for future discussions on authorship in the age of artificial intelligence.

A.4 – The decision of the Court of Appeal[4]

On September 19, 2024, Dr. Thaler filed an appeal with the United States Court of Appeals for the District of Columbia, and the appeal decision was issued on March 18, 2025, rejecting all of Thaler's arguments and further clarifying the approach of American case law on the subject of "hybrid creativity". Here is a summary of what emerged from the appeal decision.

1. First Argument Rejected: Work-Made-for-Hire
- Thaler's Argument: the Copyright Act's work-made-for-hire provision allows him to be

4 This section was added by Simone Aliprandi.

considered the "author" of the work because the Creativity Machine is his "employee".

- Court's Decision: the argument misunderstands the human authorship requirement; the Copyright Act protects only "original works of authorship" (17 U.S.C. § 102(a)); the term "authorship" necessarily refers to a human being.
- Established Principle: all "original works of authorship" must be created in the first instance by a human being, including work-made-for-hire.

2. Second Argument Rejected: Machine Ownership

- Thaler's Argument: he is the author of the work because he created and used the Creativity Machine
- Court's Decision:
  - Procedural Issue: The court cannot examine this argument on the merits.
  - Reason: Thaler waived this argument before the Copyright Office.
  - Failure to Challenge: Thaler did not challenge the district court's finding of waiver.
  - Insufficient Argument: The single sentence in the brief ("based on a misunderstanding of the record below") constitutes a "bare and conclusory assertion" insufficient to preserve the argument.

3. Final Outcome

- Complete rejection of Dr. Thaler's copyright application on both fronts: substantive (first argument) and procedural (second argument).

B – Li vs Liu (Beijing Internet Court, China, 2023)

B.1 – Points analyzed by the Court

The Beijing Internet Court examined the following key points to reach its decision.

1. Assessment of the work's copyrightability:
- The image falls within the field of visual art.
- It is the result of Li's intellectual effort, who used AI as a creative tool.
- It possesses originality, reflecting Li's creative choices in selecting and arranging visual elements.
- The use of technological tools does not preclude copyright protection, provided there is significant human creative contribution.

2. Determination of authorship:
- Li played an active role in the creative process by providing specific inputs to the AI system.
- Li exercised significant control over the AI's output through the selection of prompts, parameters, and iterations.
- Li made creative decisions in selecting and refining the final image.
- AI was used as a tool, analogous to a camera or editing software, and not as an autonomous creator.

3. Classification of the work:
- The image satisfies the criteria defined in the Implementation Regulations of the Copyright Law for fine art works.
- It is a two-dimensional visual work composed of lines and colors.
- It possesses recognizable aesthetic value.

4. Assessment of copyright infringement:
- Liu used the image without authorization, violating the right of network dissemination.
- The removal of the watermark was considered a violation of the moral right of attribution.
- Liu could not invoke ignorance of the image's source as justification.

5. Determination of sanctions:
- Liu must publish an apology to repair the damage to Li's reputation as the author.
- Compensation was established based on the difficulty of determining actual damages or illicit gain.
- The court considered the circumstances of the infringement and its impact on the rights holder.

6. Considerations regarding disclosure of AI use:
- Authors should disclose AI use, but it is not a binding legal requirement.
- Disclosure promotes transparency and allows the public to understand the creative process.
- The court recognized the importance of informing the public about new technologies used in artistic creation.

- No legal obligation was imposed, recognizing that AI is a creative tool like any other.

B.2 – Timeline of actions taken by Li

The court analyzed Li's creative process in detail, identifying the following actions.

1. Software selection:
- Li chose to use Stable Diffusion, an open-source AI software.

2. Model selection:
- Li downloaded and used two specific models:
  a) "AsiaFacemix-pruned-fix.safetensors";
  b) "lora-hanfugirl-v1-5.safetensors".

3. Text prompt configuration:
- Li composed a detailed prompt that included:
  - Artistic type: "ultra photorealistic", "color photo".
  - Subject: "japan idol" with detailed descriptions of skin, eyes, braids.
  - Setting: "in locations", "golden hour", "dynamic lighting".
  - Composition: "cool pose", "viewing at camera".
  - Style: "film texture", "film simulation".

4. Negative prompt configuration:
- Li included elements to exclude, such as "3d, render, cgi, painting, drawing, cartoon, anime, comic".

5. Technical parameter adjustment:
- Number of "iteration steps": set to 33.

- Image height: set to 768 pixels.
- "CFG scale": set to 9.
- "Random seed": initially set to 2692150200.

6. Image generation and selection:
- Li generated multiple versions of the image.
- He selected the most promising versions for further iterations.

7. Parameter modifications for subsequent iterations:
- Modified the weight of "lora-hanfugirl-v1-5.safetensors" to 0.75.
- Changed the "random seed" to 2692150199.

8. Prompt refinement:
- Added terms such as "shy, elegant, cute, lust, cool pose, teen, viewing at camera, masterpiece, best quality".

9. Final image selection:
- Li chose the final image from among hundreds generated.

10. Post-processing (mentioned but not detailed in the judgment):
- Possible use of additional software for final touch-ups.

11. Publication:
- Li published the final image on the Little Red Book social platform.

This detailed timeline of Li's actions was fundamental to the court's decision to recognize his creative contribution and, consequently, his authorship of the work generated with AI assistance.

C – Zarya of the Dawn (U.S. Copyright Office, USA, 2022)

C.1 – Aspects analyzed by the Copyright Office

The United States Copyright Office examined the following key points to reach its decision.

1. Assessment of text authorship:
- Recognition of copyright in the text as it was written entirely by Kashtanova without any AI assistance.

2. Assessment of the work's compilation:
- Recognition of copyright in the selection and arrangement of images and text, as the selection and arrangement were the product of Kashtanova's creativity.

3. Analysis of the creative process for individual images:
- Denial of copyright for individual images generated by Midjourney.
- The Copyright Office determined that it was Midjourney, not Kashtanova, who determined the expressive elements of the images.

4. Assessment of manual modifications to images:

- Denial of copyright for minor modifications made by Kashtanova.
- Rationale: the modifications were too minimal to reach the required creativity threshold.

5. Consideration of AI tool use in the creative process:
- Recognition that AI use raises new questions.
- Reaffirmation of the human authorship requirement.
- Copyright law requires human creative contribution.

6. Final decision:
- Cancellation of the original registration.
- Issuance of a new limited registration.
- Rationale: copyright law protects only the human authorship elements of the work.

C.2 – Analysis of actions taken by Kris Kashtanova

The Copyright Office analyzed the following actions by Kashtanova in the creative process.

1. Creation of textual prompts for Midjourney:
- Considered as instructions to the AI, not direct creative expression.
- AI interprets these prompts freely, so there is no direct control over the final result.

2. Selection of images generated by Midjourney:
- Considered insufficient to establish authorship.

- The fundamental creative expression comes from the AI, not from Kashtanova.

3. Iteration and refinement of prompts:
- Despite the iterative process, AI remains the primary source of visual expression.
- Prompt refinement was viewed as guidance, not direct creation.

4. Minor modifications to images using Photoshop:
- Judged too minimal to reach the creativity threshold necessary for copyright protection.

5. Arrangement and composition of images in the work:
- Recognized as worthy of copyright, but only as a compilation, not for individual images.

6. Selection of technical parameters for image generation:
- Considered technical inputs, not creative expression sufficient to establish authorship.

7. Combination of elements from different Midjourney iterations:
- Although this process requires creative choices, the office determined that the fundamental expression still came from the AI, not from Kashtanova.

8. Description of the creative process and artistic intention:

- Demonstrates Kashtanova's conceptual input, but not considered sufficient to establish authorship over AI-generated images.

9. Cropping and framing of final images:
- Recognized as part of the copyright-protected compilation, but not sufficient to establish authorship over individual images.

C.3 – Additional considerations

- The Copyright Office emphasized that the lack of predictable and direct control over the final outcome of AI-generated images is a crucial factor in denying copyright for individual images.
- The decision highlights the distinction between using AI as an assistive tool and as the primary creator of content.
- The case has stimulated broader debate about the need to update copyright laws to address the challenges posed by generative AI technologies.

This detailed analysis of Kashtanova's actions and the Copyright Office's considerations offers an in-depth view of the legal and creative complexities involved in creating works with the assistance of generative AI.

D – Biancheri vs RAI (Supreme Court of Cassation, Italy, 2023)

D.1 – Timeline of legal proceedings

1. Court of Genoa:
- Established Biancheri's authorship of the work.
- Recognized copyright infringement by RAI.
- Ordered RAI to pay damages (€40,000).
- Ordered removal of the program from RAI's website and publication of the judgment.

2. Court of Appeals of Genoa:
- Confirmed attribution of the work to Biancheri.
- Confirmed the creative character of the work.
- Recognized the commercial nature of the Sanremo Festival.
- Confirmed the timeliness of Biancheri's response.
- Confirmed the amount of compensation established at first instance.

3. Supreme Court of Cassation (2023):
- Rejected RAI's appeal.
- Confirmed the decisions of the lower courts.
- Ordered RAI to pay legal costs.
- Confirmed the €40,000 compensation in favor of Biancheri.

D.2 – Key points examined by the Court

1. Authorship of the work:
- Recognition of Biancheri as the author of the work "The scent of the night".

- Assessment of the creative process, including consideration of advanced software use (Apophysis).

2. Creative character of the work:
- Analysis of the artistic reworking performed by Biancheri.
- Distinction between simple reproduction and original artistic creation.

3. Use of generative software:
- Consideration of Apophysis use in the creative process.
- Assessment of the software's impact on the work's creativity.

4. Copyright infringement:
- Analysis of unauthorized use of the work by RAI.
- Assessment of the commercial context (Sanremo Festival).

5. Timeliness of response:
- Examination of the promptness with which Biancheri acted to protect her rights.

6. Amount of compensation:
- Assessment of damages suffered and determination of compensation amount.

D.3 – Considerations by the Supreme Court of Cassation

1. Inadmissibility of RAI's appeal:

- The appeal regarding the algorithmically generated image was declared inadmissible for procedural reasons.

2. Assessment of the creative process:
- The Court emphasized the need for thorough analysis to determine the impact of software use on the artist's creativity.

3. Compatibility between software use and creativity:
- The Court recognized that using software to generate images does not automatically exclude the possibility of creative elaboration.

4. Need for factual determination:
- The importance of verifying to what extent the use of technological tools influenced the artist's creative process was highlighted.

D.4 – Implications for the use of advanced technologies in artistic creation

1. Recognition of technology-mediated creativity:
- The judgment suggests that the use of advanced software does not preclude recognition of human creativity and authorship.

2. Importance of the creative process:
- The courts gave weight to the artistic elaboration process, a principle potentially applicable to works created with generative AI.

3. Case-by-case evaluation:
- The judgment emphasizes the need for thorough analysis of the artist's creative contribution in each individual case.

4. Openness to new forms of creativity:
- Recognition of authorship in this case may pave the way for more inclusive interpretations of works created with emerging technologies, including AI.

5. Balance between innovation and copyright:
- The decision demonstrates the legal system's attempt to adapt to new technological realities while maintaining fundamental copyright principles.

This detailed analysis of the Biancheri vs RAI case offers an in-depth view of the legal and creative complexities involved in creating works with the assistance of advanced technologies, providing an important precedent for future discussions on authorship in the digital age and generative AI era.

Sources and readings for further study

Articles, essays and commentaries

Martin Adams, *Thomson Reuters v. ROSS: the first AI fair use ruling fails to persuade*, 13 February 2025; https://www.authorsalliance.org/2025/02/13/thomson-reuters-v-ross-the-first-ai-fair-use-ruling-fails-to-persuade/.

Jacob Axelrad, *US government: Monkey selfies ineligible for copyright*, 22 August 2014, https://www.csmonitor.com/Technology/Tech-Culture/2014/0822/US-government-Monkey-selfies-ineligible-for-copyright.

Francesco Bardozzo, *Generazioni generative italiane*, in Roberto Manfredi (editor), *La musica del futuro. Lo scenario artificiale*, Tempesta Editore, 2023.

Ryan Browne, *Getty Images spending millions to battle a 'world of rhetoric' in AI suit, CEO says*, 28 May 2025, https://www.cnbc.com/2025/05/28/getty-ceo-stability-ai-lawsuit-doesnt-cover-industry-mass-theft.html.

Arlo Canella, *Quando riprodurre lo stile altrui è plagio?*, 3 June 2024, https://www.canellacamaiora.it/quando-riprodurre-lo-stile-altrui-e-plagio/.

Roberto Caso, *La società della mercificazione e della sorveglianza: dalla persona ai dati. Casi e problemi di diritto civile*, Ledizioni, 2021.

Laura Chimienti, *Diritto di Autore 4.0. L'intelligenza artificiale crea?*, Pacini Editore, 2020.

Massimo Chiriatti, Marianna Ganapini, Enrico Panai, Mario Ubiali, Giuseppe Riva, *The case for human-AI interaction as System 0 thinking*, in *Nature Human Behaviour* 8, 1829–1830 (2024).

Andrew R. Chow, *How the Disney-Midjourney Lawsuit Could Reshape the Battle Over AI and Copyright*, 11 June 2025, https://time.com/7293362/disney-universal-midjourney-lawsuit-ai/.

Andy Clark and David J. Chalmers, *The Extended Mind*, in *Analysis*, vol. 58, n. 1, January 1998.

Harold Cohen, *Driving the creative machine*, Orcas Center, Crossroads Lecture Series, 2010, https://www.aaronshome.com/aaron/publications/orcastalk2s.pdf.

Krista L. Cox, *Text and Data Mining and Fair Use in the United States*, FOSTER/Association of Research Libraries, 2015, https://www.fosteropenscience.eu/content/text-and-data-mining-and-fair-use-united-states.

Paolo Dalprato, *Creatività ibrida. Autore e opera nell'era delle macchine intelligenti*, Ledizioni, 2025.

Paolo Dalprato, *Licenze AI Generativa: guida essenziale per professionisti*, 2 September 2024; https://www.ai4business.it/intelligenza-artificiale/licenze-ai-generativa-guida-essenziale-per-professionisti/.

Giusy De Vitis, *Se l'intelligenza è artificiale, la musica è vera?,* 27 October 2021, https://www.filodiritto.com/se-lintelligenza-e-artificiale-la-musica-e-vera.

Dreyfus Law Firm, *Getty Images (US) Inc and Others v. Stability AI Ltd [2025] EWHC 38 (Ch): An interesting case in AI and Intellectual Property Law*, 19 February 2025, https://www.dreyfus.fr/en/2025/02/19/getty-images-us-inc-and-others-v-stability-ai-ltd-2025-ewhc-38-ch-an-interesting-case-in-ai-and-intellectual-property-law/.

Giovanni d'Ammassa, *Le opere tutelate*, 3 January 2014, https://www.dirittodautore.it/la-guida-al-diritto-dautore/loggetto-del-diritto-dautore/.

Larry A. DiMatteo, Cristina Poncibò, Michel Cannarsa (editors), *The Cambridge Handbook of Artificial Intelligence. Global Perspectives on Law and Ethics*, Cambridge University Press, 2022, https://doi.org/10.1017/9781009072168.

Gualtiero Dragotti, *Generative AI and prompt protection under intellectual property law*, 2025, https://www.dlapiper.com/en-us/insights/publications/law-in-tech/generative-ai-and-prompt-protection-under-intellectual-property-law.

Alfredo Esposito, *Toward a hybrid copyright for AI-Generated works the U.S. Copyright Office decision*, 6 March 2023; https://www.alfredoesposito.eu/2023/03/06/toward-a-hybrid-copyright-for-ai-generated-works-the-u-s-copyright-office-decision/.

Alfredo Esposito, *The Evolution of Hybrid Copyright: A Legal Analysis of AI-Generated Works from Zarya to Rose Enigma (2023-2025)*, 6 February 2025, https://www.alfredoesposito.eu/2025/02/06/hybrid-copyrigh-from-zarya-of-the-dawn-to-rose-enigma/.

Nicholas Gervassis and Alina Trapova, *UKIPO's public consultation on AI and IP – computer-generated works (Part 1)*, https://copyrightblog.kluweriplaw.com/2022/03/14/ukipos-public-consultation-on-ai-and-ip-computer-generated-works-part-1/.

Douglas R. Hofstadter, *Gödel, Escher, Bach: an eternal golden braid*, Basic Books, 1979, https://archive.org/details/GEBen_201706/.

Thomas James, *AI OK; Piracy Not: Bartz v. Anthropic*, 25 June 2025, https://thomasbjames.com/ai-ok-piracy-not-bartz-v-anthropic/.

Daniel Kahneman, *Thinking, Fast and Slow*, Straus and Giroux, 2011.

Garry Kasparov, *Deep Thinking: Where Machine Intelligence Ends and Human Creativity Begins*, PublicAffairs, 2017.

Edward Lee, *Studio Ghibli v. OpenAI: is this the next U.S. copyright lawsuit to drop?*, 28 March 2025, https://chatgptiseatingtheworld.com/2025/03/28/ghibli-studios-v-openai-is-this-next-u-s-copyright-lawsuit-to-drop/.

Jyh-An Lee, Reto Hilty, Kung-Chung Liu (editors), *Artificial Intelligence and Intellectual Property*, Oxford University Press, 2021, https://academic.oup.com/book/39560/chapter/339432200, DOI 10.1093/oso/9780198870944.001.0001.

Lawrence Lessig, *The Future of Ideas: The Fate of the Commons in a Connected World*, Random House, 2001, https://dlc.dlib.indiana.edu/dlcrest/api/core/bitstreams/9f04771b-cd83-4b47-967c-60865382dda7/content.

Lawrence Lessig, *Free Culture: How Big Media Uses Technology and the Law to Lock Down Culture and Control Creativity*, Penguin Books, 2004, https://en.wikipedia.org/wiki/Free_Culture_(book).

Madison Malone Kircher, *People Love Studio Ghibli. But Should They Be Able to Recreate It?*, 27 March 2025, https://www.nytimes.com/2025/03/27/style/ai-chatgpt-studio-ghibli.html.

Jim Mann, *How an American author tested the copyright laws for AI generated content*, 30 April 2024, https://lawdit.co.uk/readingroom/how-an-american-author-tested-the-copyright-laws-for-ai-generated-content.

Paolo Marinoni, *AI debole e forte: differenze concettuali e limiti*, 24 May 2022, https://ainews.it/ai-debole-e-forte-differenze-concettuali-e-limiti/.

Atreya Mathur, *A Rose Enigma: Pending (Right) Protection*, 8 December 2023, https://itsartlaw.org/2023/12/08/rose-enigma/.

Atreya Mathur, *Copyright Registration for AI Generated Works: Zarya of the Dawn and the Dawn of a New Creator*, 6 July 2023, https://itsartlaw.org/2023/07/06/copyright-registration-for-ai-generated-works-zarya-of-the-dawn-and-the-dawn-of-a-new-creator/.

Aaron Moss, *Artists Attack AI: Why The New Lawsuit Goes Too Far*, 23 January 2023, https://copyrightlately.com/artists-copyright-infringement-lawsuit-ai-art-tools/.

Andrea Monti, *The Digital Rights Delusion. Humans, Machines and the Technology of Information*, Routledge India, 2023.

Rachel Muller-Heyndyk, *Daniel Susskind: The AI fallacy*, 18 February 2019, https://www.hrmagazine.co.uk/content/news/daniel-susskind-the-ai-fallacy/.

Tim O'Reilly, *You Can't Regulate What You Don't Understand. Or, Why AI Regulations Should Begin with Mandated Disclosures*, 15 June 2023, https://www.oreilly.com/radar/you-cant-regulate-what-you-dont-understand/.

Eric Steven Raymond, *The cathedral and the bazaar*, http://www.catb.org/~esr/writings/cathedral-bazaar/.

Rob Salkowitz, *Midjourney Founder David Holz On The Impact Of AI On Art, Imagination And The Creative Economy*, 16 Septembner 2022, https://www.forbes.com/sites/robsalkowitz/2022/09/16/midjourney-founder-david-holz-on-the-impact-of-ai-on-art-imagination-and-the-creative-economy/?sh=628200a72d2b.

Daniel Susskind, *A World Without Work. Technology, Automation, and How We Should Respond*, Metropolitan Books, 2020.

Peter Swirski, *From literature tu biterature. Lem, Turing, Darwin, and Explorations in Computer Literature, Philosophy of Mind, and Cultural Evolution*, McGill-Queen's University Press, 2013.

James Vincent, *AI art tools Stable Diffusion and Midjourney targeted with copyright lawsuit*, 16 January 2023, https://www.theverge.com/2023/1/16/23557098/generative-ai-art-copyright-legal-lawsuit-stable-diffusion-midjourney-deviantart.

James Vincent, *Getty Images is suing the creators of AI art tool Stable Diffusion for scraping its content*, 17 January 2023, https://www.theverge.com/2023/1/17/23558516/ai-art-copyright-stable-diffusion-getty-images-lawsuit.

Geraint A. Wiggins, *Searching for computational creativity*, in *New Generation Computing*, vol. 24, n. 3, 2006, pp. 209-222.

Roosa Wingström, Johanna Hautala & Riina Lundman, *Redefining Creativity in the Era of AI? Perspectives of Computer Scientists and New Media Artists*, in *Creativity Research Journal*, 2024, VOL. 36, NO. 2, 177–193, DOI https://doi.org/10.1080/10400419.2022.2107850.

Court decisions and other official documents

Compendium of United States Copyright Office Practices, 3rd edition, 2014, https://copyright.gov/comp3/docs/compendium.pdf.

Copyright Registration Guidance: Works Containing Material Generated by Artificial Intelligence, United States Copyright Office Practices, March 2023; https://aliprandi.blogspot.com/2023/03/copyright-office-usa-esprime-creazioni-generate-intelligenza-artificiale.html.

Decisions J 8/20 of the Legal Board of Appeal about the "Designation of inventor/DABUS" case, EPO European Patent Office; 21 December 2021; https://www.epo.org/law-practice/case-law-appeals/recent/j200008eu1.html.

Decision in the case between Stephen Thaler (Plaintiff) vs US Patent Trademark Office (Defendant), US District Court for the Eastern District of Virginia, [DABUS case – Case 1:20-cv-00903-LMB-TCB]; 2 September 2021; https://zenodo.org/records/14995418.

Decision in the case between Getty Images and others (Claimants) vs Stability AI (Defendant) [Neutral Citation Number: [2025] EWHC 38 (Ch) | Case No: IL-2023-000007], Royal Courts of Justice of the United Kingdom; published on 14 January 2025; https://zenodo.org/records/14993002.

Decision and order by Judge McMahon in the case between Raw Story Media & AlterNet Media (Plaintiffs) vs OpenAI (Defendant), United States District Court – Southern District of New York; 7 November 2024; https://zenodo.org/records/14317998.

Decision (order) by the United States District Court - Northern District of California for the case between A. Bartz, C. Graeber, K. Wallace Johnson (Plaintiffs) and Anthropic (Defendant); 23 June 2025; https://zenodo.org/records/15847017.

Decision by the United States Court of Appeals for the District of Columbia Circuit for the case between S. Thaler (Appellant) and S. Perlmutter / US Copyright Office (Appellees); 18 March 2025; https://zenodo.org/records/15847247.

Memorandum Opinion by Judge Beryl A. Howel for the case between Stephen Thaler vs U.S. Copyright Office, United States District Court – District of Columbia (Washington); 18 August 2023; https://zenodo.org/records/8268001.

Memorandum Opinion by Judge Bibas for the case between Thomson Reuters vs ROSS Intelligence, United States District Court – District of Delaware; 5 February 2025; https://zenodo.org/records/14936656.

Order on motion to dismiss and strike by Judge William H. Orrick in the case Andersen et al. (Plaintiffs) vs Stablity AI et al. (Defendants), United States District Court – Northern District of California; 30 October 2023; https://zenodo.org/records/10072494.

Order denying the plaintiffs' motion for partial summary judgment and granting Meta's cross-motion for partial summary judgment in the case between R. Kadrey (Plaintiff) vs. Meta Platforms (Defendant); 25 June 2025; https://zenodo.org/records/15847228.

Ordinanza by Supreme Court of Cassation (First Civil Section) N. 1107/2023, 16 January 2023; https://aliprandi.blogspot.com/2023/04/ordinanza-rai-utilizzo-immagine-AI-scenografia-sanremo2016.html.

European Parliament resolution of 20 October 2020 with recommendations to the Commission on a civil liability regime for artificial intelligence, https://eur-lex.europa.eu/legal-content/EN/TXT/?uri=oj:JOC_2021_404_R_0006.

European Parliament resolution of 20 October 2020 with recommendations to the Commission on a framework of ethical aspects of artificial intelligence, robotics and related technologies, https://eur-lex.europa.eu/legal-content/EN/TXT/?uri=oj:JOC_2021_404_R_0005.

European Parliament resolution of 20 October 2020 on intellectual property rights for the development of artificial intelligence technologies, https://www.europarl.europa.eu/doceo/document/TA-9-2020-0277_EN.html.

White papers and project reports

Commission Guidelines on prohibited artificial intelligence practices established by Regulation (EU) 2024/1689 (AI Act), 4 February 2025, https://digital-strategy.ec.europa.eu/en/library/commission-publishes-guidelines-prohibited-artificial-intelligence-ai-practices-defined-ai-act.

Communia Association, Policy Paper #15 on using copyrighted works for teaching the machine, https://communia-association.org/2023/04/26/using-copyrighted-works-for-teaching-the-machine-new-policy-paper/.

Copyright and Artificial Intelligence. Part 1: Digital replicas, United States Copyright Office, July 2024, https://www.copyright.gov/ai/.

Copyright and Artificial Intelligence. Part 2: Copyrightability, United States Copyright Office, January 2025, https://www.copyright.gov/ai/.

Copyright and Artificial Intelligence. Part 3: Generative AI Training, United States Copyright Office, May 2025, https://www.copyright.gov/ai/.

Copyright and Generative AI: Opinion of the European Copyright Society, CREATe working paper 2025/1, ECS, January 2025, https://european-copyrightsociety.org/wp-content/uploads/2025/02/ecs_opinion_genai_january2025.pdf.

Creative Industries and GenAI by IFOW for the Crafting Responsive Assessments of AI & Tech-Impacted Futures (CREAATIF) research project, 4 June 2025, https://www.ifow.org/publications/executive-summary-creative-industries.

Exploratory note on Privacy, Data Protection and Large Language Models by DSCI/NASSCOM, 9 June 2023, https://www.dsci.in/resource/content/exploratory-note-privacy-data-protection-and-large-language-models.

EU AI Act Handbook by White & Case LLP, 22 May 2025, https://www.whitecase.com/insight-alert/white-case-launches-eu-ai-act-handbook.

Generative AI Outlook Report. Exploring the Intersection of Technology, Society and Policy, by European Commission (Publications Office of the European Union), 13 June 2025, https://publications.jrc.ec.europa.eu/repository/handle/JRC142598.

Global Artificial Intelligence Report (2025) by IDC-A, June 2025, https://www.idc-a.org/insights/obKr4NJQdK5sYcAQaGZD.

Global Trends in AI Governance: Evolving Country Approaches, by World Bank Group, 12 May 2024, https://openknowledge.worldbank.org/entities/publication/a570d81a-0b48-4cac-a3d9-73dff48a8f1a.

Intellectual property issues in artificial intelligence trained on scraped data, OECD Artificial Intelligence Papers, February 2025 No. 33, https://www.oecd.org/en/publications/intellectual-property-issues-in-artificial-intelligence-trained-on-scraped-data_d5241a23-en.html.

Privacy and Data Protection Risks in Large Language Models (LLMs), by Isabel Barberá and Murielle Popa-Fabre for the Consultative Committee of the Convention for the Protection of Individuals with Regard to Automatic Processing of Personal Data (Convention 108); Expert Report prepared for presentation to the 48th Plenary meeting, 17 June 2025; https://rm.coe.int/privacy-and-data-protection-risks-in-large-language-models-llms-v1-0/1680b631dd.

Responsible Use of Generative AI. A Playbook for Product Managers & Business Leaders, by U.C. Berkeley AI Research Lab, 2025, https://re-ai.berkeley.edu/projects/responsible-use-generative-ai.

Sharing trustworthy AI models with privacy-enhancing technologies, policy paper by OECD, 17 June 2025, https://www.oecd.org/en/publications/sharing-trustworthy-ai-models-with-privacy-enhancing-technologies_a266160b-en.html.

Skills in the Age of AI, report by cross-party think tank Policy Connect, 16 June 2025, https://www.policyconnect.org.uk/research/skills-age-ai.

The development of generative artificial intelligence from a copyright perspective, European Union Intellectual Property Office (EUIPO), 2025, https://www.euipo.europa.eu/en/publications/genai-from-a-copyright-perspective-2025.

Volume of data/information created, captured, copied, and consumed worldwide from 2010 to 2023, with forecasts from 2024 to 2028, disponibile all'URL https://www.statista.com/statistics/871513/worldwide-data-created/.

Other works by the author on this and related topics (all are freely available online, many under Creative Commons licenses)

Simone Aliprandi, *L'autore artificiale 2. Creatività e proprietà intellettuale nell'era dell'AI*, Ledizioni, 2025 (Italian version of this book); https://aliprandi.org/books/autore-artificiale2/.

Simone Aliprandi (editor), *Il design nell'era della creatività artificiale. Nuove sfide per la progettazione e la didattica*, Ledizioni, 2024 (contributors: Simone Aliprandi, Serena Bedini, Francesco Bonomi, Rosa Maria Di Giorgi, Francesco Fumelli, Maurizio Galluzzo,

Antonio Glessi, Francesca Parotti, Simone Paternich, Marco E. Romano, Chiara Rubessi); https://aliprandi.org/books/design-era-creativita-artificiale/.

Simone Aliprandi, *Software licensing & data governance. Tutelare e gestire le creazioni tecnologiche*, Apogeo, 2020; https://aliprandi.org/books/software-licensing-data-governance/.

Simone Aliprandi, *Creative Commons: a user guide*, Ledizioni, 2013; https://aliprandi.org/books/cc-user-guide/.

Simone Aliprandi, *Oscar Wilde, diritto d'autore e intelligenza artificiale*, in *Apogeonline.com*; https://www.apogeonline.com/articoli/oscar-wilde-diritto-dautore-e-intelligenza-artificiale-simone-aliprandi/.

Simone Aliprandi and Carlo Piana, *Tutela dei beni culturali e lo strano caso di Studi d'arte Cave Michelangelo*, 2023; https://aliprandi.blogspot.com/2023/02/beni-culturali-caso-studi-arte-cave-michelangelo-commento-ordinanza.html.

Simone Aliprandi, *AI Act: cosa dicono le norme sul diritto d'autore*, 26 March 2024; https://www.ai4business.it/intelligenza-artificiale/ai-act-cosa-dicono-le-norme-sul-diritto-dautore/.

Simone Aliprandi, *The Future of Copyright in the Age of Artificial Creativity*, 28 October 2024; https://www.aracneai.com/the-future-of-copyright-in-the-age-of-artificial-creativity-with-simone-aliprandi/ (an interview collected by Francesco Cerisano for the website Aracneai.com).

Simone Aliprandi, *AI, copyright e moda: qualche riflessione alla luce del caso Shein*, 24 October 2024; https://www.youtube.com/playlist?list=PLYoUkCOw_SXjLVOM7Zaimo2DeUD6aYQ9Y (video lesson).

Simone Aliprandi, *AI: tentativi di regolamentazione e qualche spunto giurisprudenziale in ambito copyright*, 27 February 2025; https://youtube.com/playlist?list=PLYoUkCOw_SXiwwO4rwBzAFMSl6DjC1SN&si=39XLWq3CDeTvZaWp (video lesson)

www.ingramcontent.com/pod-product-compliance
Lightning Source LLC
LaVergne TN
LVHW050928210926
848482LV00013B/574

9791256004898